Tea *and* Dog Biscuits

OUR FIRST TOPSY-TURVY YEAR FOSTERING ORPHAN DOGS

Barrie Hawkins

CHICAGO
REVIEW
PRESS

Cover design: Sarah Olson
Cover images: dog, Waldemar Dabrowski/Shutterstock; landscape,
John Woodworth/Photodisc/Getty Images

This edition published in 2010 by Chicago Review Press
Published by arrangement with Summersdale Publishers Ltd.
© 2009 by Barrie Hawkins
All rights reserved

Chicago Review Press, Incorporated
814 North Franklin Street
Chicago, Illinois 60610
ISBN 978-1-56976-341-4
Printed in the United States of America
5 4 3 2 1

*This book is dedicated to Gerry Robinson,
who helps animals when others pass by*

Author's Note

Tea and Dog Biscuits is an account of real events, but identities, locations and some details have necessarily been changed for reasons of privacy and confidentiality.

Contents

Squashing the Daisies

'He was a guard dog.'

'A guard dog!' I repeated.

'In a car breakers' yard in the East End,' Cecilia added.

I stood in silent contemplation for several moments as the implications of that piece of information sank in. A couple of months earlier my wife and I had decided to help dogs that needed a home. Since then we had taken in a few – this would be the seventh orphan – but the others had all been family pets.

'Was a guard dog... How long ago?' I asked.

'Two or three hours,' Cecilia replied.

I stood in silent contemplation again, this time with my mouth open.

Where's Dorothy? I thought. This would happen when Dorothy isn't here. My wife was usually there to take charge when the dogs came in.

Cecilia was looking at me intently. I felt I was beginning to look hesitant in front of her and needed to offer an explanation.

'Dorothy mostly handles the dogs,' I said. 'I deal with the people.' At least, that was the plan.

'I bet you he's a poppet,' Cecilia said.

I turned and looked at the former parcel-delivery van in which Cecilia had brought the dog. I remembered that she'd always had a Volvo and I asked her what had happened to it. I think I was filling in time, putting off the moment before we had to open the back door of that van.

'He's too big to get in the Volvo estate,' Cecilia said.

I looked up to the heavens.

Cecilia forced a smile. 'Only joking, Barrie. The engine seized. They said I'd never put any oil in it.'

I had the suspicion that this was her way of preparing me.

She turned to the van. 'Isn't he quiet in there?' She turned back to give me another smile, this time a reassuring one. 'He could be so laid-back he's gone to sleep.'

In her urge to reassure me Cecilia was losing sight of reality: despite not doing rescue work for long, I knew enough to know the dog was not going to be having a snooze.

I went to the back of the Transit van to try to get a glimpse of what Cecilia had brought us, but somebody had painted the windows black.

'He is tied in, isn't he?' I asked.

I had already learned some valuable lessons about handling strange dogs. One of them was that if you open the door of a vehicle with a dog inside it is likely to leap out – and, in our circumstances, run off. I had learnt that when a dog comes to us, Safety First dictates that the dog should be secured in the vehicle used to bring him. Especially if he is not brought to us by his owner – as in this case.

Cecilia shook her head and endeavoured to look contrite. 'I know he should have been, Barrie, but...' Her voice trailed off.

'But what?'

'I meant to – I know it's a lot safer – but I didn't put him in the van.'

'You didn't put him in?' This was an interesting piece of information.

'No, the men at the yard put him in.'

'So you haven't handled this dog, Cecilia?'

She shook her head again.

'I can't deal with big dogs, Barrie, I only want to rescue Yorkies and littlies. That's why I brought him to you.'

Now she put on the pleading voice, a voice that I was going to hear many times in the future, had I but known it.

'Oh please, Barrie, please take him. I don't know what I'll do if you don't take him.'

She took hold of a strand of her long unbrushed hair, twiddled it round a finger and hung her head. A woman who, when it came to rescuing dogs, had single-handedly chased an armed gang of illegal hare coursers, now managed to look helpless.

'You did leave his lead on him,' I said. It wasn't a question.

Having done rescue work for years, she would know that it's easier to catch a dog if it has a trailing lead you can jump on. This prevents having to grab the dog, which is not to be recommended if you are a stranger and it is a large dog.

I had a comforting thought: Dorothy will be home soon. Then I remembered that she would be going after work to join Jolly Jumpers, a trampolining class. I couldn't ask her to miss the first class. She would be having fun leaping about on a trampoline while I was leaping about trying to grab hold of a big dog I'd never met before.

'It's Dorothy that mostly deals with the dogs,' I said.

'Yes, I know. You said before.'

I sighed.

There was nothing else for it but to get him out.

'OK,' I said. 'We'll just have to open the door and grab his lead so that he can't run off.' I hadn't noticed that Cecilia had remained silent when I spoke about the lead. 'But as he doesn't know us he might hang back – if he does, I'll call his name.' I marched across to the van.

Cecilia stayed where she was.

I put my hands on my hips. 'Come on, Cecilia. You've got to help. I can't do it on my own.'

She walked slowly across to join me. Now I was at the van doors I had butterflies in my tummy and her reluctance was adding to their number.

'What's his name?' I asked.

Cecilia shook her head.

'You don't know the dog's name!'

'Don't get angry with me, Barrie.'

'Cecilia, how did you manage not to even ask his name?'

'He hasn't got one.'

I fell silent.

'He's never had a name, Barrie. He's just been "the dog".'

Cecilia had stopped me in my tracks. They never even gave him a name? Surely nobody would have a dog and not give him a name.

'Hadn't they had him long then?' I asked eventually.

'They've had him years. He's a big mature male.'

The van had twin back doors. My hand halfway to the handle of one of them, I paused. A dog of mature years is much less likely to take instructions from a stranger. He is much more likely to be confident and assertive.

'And Barrie...' Cecilia screwed up her face to break painful news. 'He hasn't got a collar on.'

It took me a while before I could speak. 'You are *joking*! How do I get hold of him when we get him out?'

Cecilia shook her head. 'They've never had a collar on him.'

I sighed again. Not even a collar! I could feel my forehead was damp with sweat.

Cecilia took hold of my arm. 'Barrie, the man grabbed his mane – he's got the biggest mane I've ever seen on a dog. Oh, and Barrie – he's got a huge chest and this enormous neck. And that wonderful mane is almost ginger.' She nodded enthusiastically. 'He's like a lion.'

I sighed again. The longer I put it off, the worse it would be. I took hold of the handle on the back door. No sound came from within. I tightened my grip on the door handle and hesitated.

It was then that Cecilia pulled the other door open. Something flew past me at head height, something mostly dark, a blur of fur. I managed somehow to stop myself falling over backwards onto the gravel, straightened up, stared into the empty van for a second then jerked round to see where the blur had gone.

It was standing in the middle of the lawn.

A big dog. A very, very big dog.

'Barrie, look at that gorgeous mane. Have you ever seen anything like that? Don't you think it's like a lion's?'

I did.

The Lion-Maned Dog stood, a solid, motionless mass, in the middle of the lawn, four feet planted on the grass, squashing the daisies. He stood there, staring.

I had started the rescue work because I loved dogs, especially big dogs, and German Shepherds (the breed that used to be known as Alsatians) in particular. Before me stood a magnificent example of that breed.

He was not looking around to see where he had been brought to, as I would have expected. He was looking at me. If it is possible for a dog to have a glint in his eye, then this dog did. He stared at the pale-faced, bespectacled male with middle-age spread, and I could tell what he was thinking. He didn't see me as a challenge.

I can't do this, I thought. But I had to. I had a dog to whom I was a stranger, a guard dog out of a car breakers' yard, with no name and no collar and no lead and somehow or other I had to get hold of this dog and put him in one of our dog pens so that he and other people would be safe.

On a warm, sunny Tuesday afternoon our tiny village felt lazy and peaceful. No pedestrians and few vehicles had passed by since Cecilia's van had turned into the drive. This peace and stillness was what I needed. I knew enough to realise that the Lion-Maned Dog must not get agitated or excited. I needed him to remain calm. But what to do? I quickly ran through the alternatives in my mind.

There was only one thing I could do in the circumstances.

I spoke to him.

'Good boy.'

I think I may have spoken to him too quietly: the Lion-Maned Dog apparently hadn't heard me tell him that he was a good boy. He remained standing motionless in the middle of the lawn.

When Dorothy and I would try to find a home for this dog later, breaking the news that he was a former guard dog from a car breakers' yard would not make him an easy choice for those seeking a family pet. As I stood facing the Lion-Maned Dog across the lawn I had to shut out of my own mind an image of the guard dog in our own local breakers' yard. Better not to think about how he would attempt to bend the bars with his teeth if customers approached his cage. The proprietor had once volunteered the information that German Shepherds had forty-two teeth and he thought his dog was trying to bite one person for every tooth.

Like two cowboys in a Western, this dog and I faced each other under the hot sun. Who would draw first?

I suddenly remembered that Cecilia was still with us. Without moving my head I managed to look sideways: she was a third motionless figure, a spectator. I was about to tell her in a calm voice not to make a sudden movement when she raised her arm and began jabbing a finger in the direction of the roadway. A coach was pulling up by the end of our drive, some two or three car lengths from where I stood. A coach? It came to a halt, the passenger doors opened, and a tall man in a uniform jumped out.

'Right,' he said in a loud, authoritarian voice.

A small, ginger-haired lad was the first to follow him, leaping off the step. Then the others. Squeezing out of the coach, spilling onto the pavement and the verge. Thirty? Forty?

On a Tuesday afternoon in our peaceful, isolated village – a village with no shop, no school, no pub, where the most exciting thing in the village is the pillar box, where the only people I ever see on foot are the Commander taking his dogs for a brisk walk and the vicar – a troop of Scouts landed at the end of my drive. I know very little of the modern Scouting movement and do not know whether today they go on route marches, but with their clomping boots and commanding leader the small boys certainly had a military resemblance.

My eyes swivelled round to the Lion-Maned Dog. His ears had gone up; he had turned his head to look behind him. Almost certainly he could not have seen a Scout troop before. Almost certainly it was far more human beings than he had ever seen before all at once. What would he do? Possibilities rushed into my head. Would this guard dog start barking at all these people who had suddenly appeared? Would he rush over and leap up at them? Drag them off? Savage them? Would he savage *me*?

Then the lawyer in me thought, have I used reasonable skill and taken reasonable precautions to control and secure this dog? I have not.

The last of the coach's occupants jumped out: the others were forming themselves into a column, just the other side of our low garden wall, which had shrunk since the last time I looked at it.

SQUASHING THE DAISIES

Having no children of my own I'm not very good at guessing their ages but I supposed these were Cub Scouts. They were surprisingly quiet for a large group of young boys; perhaps they had been instructed not to disturb the peace of the village residents. This may have contributed to the Lion-Maned Dog's puzzlement – I'm sure his brow was furrowed – and left him wondering how to react.

'Barrie!' I heard Cecilia speak in hushed tones. 'Barrie, he was originally a police dog. That's good – he's used to doing as he's told. Give him a command. Tell him to sit or something.'

Well, that probably is good news, I thought. Yes. She should have told me that before. Yes, that's what I'll do.

'He was definitely a police dog, they just couldn't keep him because he wouldn't let go of people once...'

Her voice trailed off. Even she realised this had not been the right moment to tell me that.

I was just about to give the dog a command when the troop leader turned and spoke to his charges.

'Ready?' he asked.

This prompted the ginger-haired lad to point at the Lion-Maned Dog in the middle of our lawn. 'What a big dog.'

The troop leader turned round and looked at the dog. Then in a booming voice he shouted, 'Right – COME ON!'

The Lion-Maned Dog spun round. His body stiffened. Oh, my goodness. Was he about to join the Scouts?

For several long, long moments he made no further movement. He gave no sign that he was interested in or disturbed by the troop leader and his invading force outside the garden.

Then suddenly he sprang off – in the opposite direction to the Scouts. I was left gawping, then turned to see his tail disappearing round the corner of the cottage. He was gone. On the loose, no lead, not even a collar.

My mouth was as dry as an old bone. I took two or three deep swallows and made off after him, taking strides as big as I could. I made it to the corner of the cottage in seconds and rounded the corner, my face screwed up. What was I going to see? What – or who – had he gone after? The gate to the back garden stood open. I shot past a large sign I had nailed to the fence when we first started taking dogs, painted in blood red: STOP! DO NOT ENTER – ALSATIAN MAY BE LOOSE IN GARDEN.

I stopped to look around. At the far end of our long garden, beyond one of the flowerbeds, I could see next door's cat running – although not seemingly in too much of a hurry – towards a gap in the hedge, followed a few yards behind by a large German Shepherd dog, also seemingly not in too much of a hurry. The cat disappeared through the gap; the German Shepherd crashed into the hedge. His head disappeared into the gap, then his body writhed and wriggled for a few seconds. He pulled his head out of the gap, shook himself, ran off along the hedge in search of a bigger gap, found it, launched himself into it, and got stuck again, but further in this time. After more wriggling he pulled himself out and set off along the hedge again to another gap. He was having fun.

Another twenty or thirty yards and there was a gap in the hedge that would be big enough to take him through into an adjoining field and freedom. Freedom to roam the village – and beyond. There are people out there in the big, wide world who have an unreasonable fear of German Shepherd dogs, who will cross the road to avoid one, or who will pick up their children or their Yorkie if one approaches. This would be his chance to meet them.

Earth, dust and dead leaves were flying up now from the current gap in the hedge, which Lion-Maned Dog was making bigger.

I put my hand to my forehead. If Dorothy were here she would say, 'Calm down. Don't panic, Mr Hawkins.' I quickly took some deep breaths. No, take s-l-o-o-o-w deep breaths.

Think! It's no good me running after the dog – he can run faster than I can. But I can't call him, he hasn't got a name. Just try calling him without a name? And look welcoming?

'Come on, boy! Here!' I called out. Lion-Maned Dog looked round momentarily then promptly ran on to the next gap. What would a dog trainer do? Or a police dog handler? And while you're thinking, walk slowly towards him.

I took two or three slow cautious steps. Lion-Maned Dog looked up and bolted on to the next gap. I didn't go any further.

Since we had started the rescue work we had become friends with a police dog handler. Now I realised the truth of what he had told us: you haven't got control of a dog unless you can get it to come. The secret, he had said, was to be more interesting than what the dog was doing. His advice was to squat down to the level of the dog, so you're not towering above him like a threatening giant. Then waggle your fingers about in the grass as if you are trying to find something.

I squatted down. Immediately, I realised that my head was about level with the dog's teeth. My movement must have caught the attention of Lion-Maned Dog; he turned his head. I put a hand down and wiggled my fingers about.

Some dogs have faces which allow you to read more easily what they are thinking. Lion-Maned Dog had such a face. And it seemed to me he was thinking, What's that idiot doing? He quickly turned back to resume his excavations of the current gap.

'Ooohhh... What's this?' I said. Then, excitedly, 'Ooohhh – look what I've found!'

Lion-Maned Dog turned his head for the briefest of looks then hurried on to the next gap. The next gap was the one big enough to provide his ticket to freedom.

In case Finding Something Interesting hasn't worked, our dog handler friend had gone on to reveal the Technique That Never Fails. He told us that he himself had only ever done this once. It had been taught to him at police dog training school as the ultimate weapon. He told us it took guts.

From the squatting-down Finding-Something-Interesting position, roll over onto your back. Stick all four arms and legs up into the air and move them all about simultaneously in a cycling motion. Think of a beetle that's rolled over onto its back and can't get up again. No dog can resist that, the handler said – he'll have to come over to see what's happened.

I rolled over onto my back in the grass. Through my shirt I could feel I had dropped onto something sticky and damp. In fear and dread that Lion-Maned Dog would disappear through the next gap and be gone to wreak havoc and terror in the village I thrashed about wildly, arms and legs flailing.

Lion-Maned Dog stopped his excavations. In fact, he froze and stood staring.

I pedalled faster. 'Good boy! Good *boy*! Look at me! What am I doing?!' But Lion-Maned Dog wasn't looking in my direction. I turned my head to follow his line of sight.

My heart must have missed a beat. There at the top of the garden stood a grey-haired lady. She held a collecting tin. She was staring at me. I scrambled to my feet. 'Go away! Can't you see the sign?' I yelled. '*Go away!*'

'It's all right. Dogs like me,' was the reply.

Lion-Maned Dog stiffened, then launched himself off in the charity woman's direction.

He was racing past on the other side of a flowerbed. Somehow, both feet at once, I sprang up into the air – and then forward. I felt myself actually sailing through the air, then down on top of him.

Sixteen stone of me came from out of the sky, landing squarely on him. He crashed to the ground, his legs splayed out to the sides.

For several seconds we both lay there motionless, me covering him completely. I looked down, resting my chin on my chest, and could see his head underneath me. I raised myself up a couple of inches to give him some air.

For a moment I thought he was dead. I lifted myself up a bit more but with my hands clasped round his neck. Then he made a sound like the noise made by a balloon when the air escapes.

'*Thhwwuuuuuuuuurrr.*'

Like a rider getting off a horse, I lifted a leg up and dismounted, still with those hands firmly round his neck. Lion-Maned Dog jumped to his feet, taking me by surprise. Then he shook himself – but I hung on. He finished his shake and just stood there, gathering his thoughts. Our eyes met.

And then the Lion-Maned Dog grinned.

This was a game. He was having fun.

His great tail swept the air. I felt my eyes glisten over with relief. Perhaps this was the first time anybody had ever played with him.

My grasp around his neck became a hug.

I had something to tell him and was about to say his name when I remembered. I paused.

'Number Seven,' I said, 'you're a good boy.'

And this time, I meant it.

In the Beginning

It had been a very long journey. The trolley had squeaked its way along what seemed to be the longest corridors I had ever seen. One lot of swing doors after another. Through a waiting area. Then a long wait for a lift. The last set of swing doors brought us into this windowless place, in which Dorothy had been trolleyed to the far end.

I turned my head to the right. A very old man, his face all wrinkles, awaited his turn on another trolley, unmoving, eyes closed. During the weeks Dorothy had been in hospital, most of the patients on her ward had been so elderly it had made me ask the resentful question, Why should this happen to her at this age? So I looked away from the very old man.

Turning away to the left took my gaze to a wall painted for its entire run of some forty or fifty feet with a mural. I found myself staring at Mickey Mouse.

I blinked at him. Are they mad? Why on earth have they painted the wall outside an operating theatre with scenes from Disney? The people here are waiting for serious surgery. Then I realised it had been painted for the sake of the children. I remembered that the hospital was famous for its work with youngsters as well as the kind of work they were doing for my Dorothy. They would have had lots of children in this room, waiting.

I lifted Dorothy's hand towards the mural. 'Look,' I said.

She turned her head. 'Have you only just seen it?' She smiled at me. 'How could you not see that?'

It was giving us something to talk about.

'There's Pluto,' Dorothy said.

Mickey Mouse was not her favourite Disney character but we both liked Pluto, who for some reason had been drawn bigger than the other characters, with huge friendly eyes.

'Oh, yes,' I said. I didn't know much about Pluto and tried to think of something to say about him. I wanted to talk about anything except the operation Dorothy was about to have.

'He looks like my dog,' said a voice from behind us. I turned. The very old man's head was tilted to one side now and his eyes were open, fixed on the mural. He had come alive.

'Does he?' I said, to keep the conversation going. This was a welcome interruption.

'What's his name?' Dorothy asked the man. I knew immediately that her motive was to take his mind off things. There was nobody with him.

There came a very long pause.

'I can't remember,' said the man. Then another long pause. 'Oh yes,' he suddenly said. 'Elton.'

'Oh. That's unusual,' I said.

'Daft name,' he responded. 'My grand-daughter called him after that singer.'

'Oh, Elton John,' I said. The conversation was lit now.

'No.'

'Oh.'

'Elton Presley.'

Dorothy and I couldn't help but smile at one another. The very old man closed his eyes. He had given up on trying to converse with me.

A woman encased in full theatre gear, accompanied by two men, came through a pair of swing doors that broke up the mural.

The woman rustled across to the old man and spoke quietly to him. One of the men released the brake on the old man's trolley and with his colleague pulled it to the swing doors. The woman paused to say to us, 'We'll be with you in a couple of minutes, Mrs Hawkins.'

She knows Dorothy's name, I thought. I was always grateful when they used my wife's name. If they used her name it seemed as if she mattered more. It was an enormous hospital, like a small town, and there was the anxiety that you were just one of a mass of patients. But the staff worked against that. There had been worrying stories in the newspapers about the state of the National Health Service but they bore no relation to what we had seen. The images we had grown up with and held all our lives of knowledgeable doctors and kind, smiling nurses had come to life.

Any isolated lapses had been more than made up for by the reassurance of all the professionals we had met: the quiet, calm voices; the seemingly unhurried manner, especially the doctors; the young lady doctor who had so patiently talked us through all the alternatives to what was going to happen; the surgeon who had crept into the ward late at night, unexpected after his twelve-hour shift in the operating theatre, to sit on my wife's bed, chatting to her quietly for half an hour the night before her operation, before going home at last for his evening meal.

I was recalling all this in the silence that had returned after the swing doors had banged together, eating up the old man.

I was squeezing Dorothy's hand and I stared into her eyes. In comparison with most people her green eyes seem unusually big, or it may be that she is often wide-eyed like a little girl. My own eyes were wet.

I felt privileged that she had chosen me to be her husband. In the months past I had often wished that I could just lift the pain off her, even if only for a while. That we could have passed it backwards and forwards between us when it became too much, that we could have shared it like we had shared everything else.

With only a couple of minutes to go, the time had come to reassure Dorothy, although I knew that, typically, she would be more worried about me than about herself. I couldn't start with what I wanted to say, so I said instead, 'It's true, you know – you should have been a nurse. You have an angelic face, my Dorothy. If it was me that was in hospital and I opened my eyes and saw you, I would think I had died and gone to heaven.' Without meaning it the dreaded word had come into the conversation. Now I was prompted to say what I had to.

'If... if this doesn't work out... I won't do anything silly. I'll keep myself busy. I won't waste my life.'

'You'll find somebody else. You must get remarried.'

'That's not going to happen,' I said.

We were both crying.

This was more than two minutes. Is it going to be delayed again? We had never got this far before. I closed my eyes and memories from the last few weeks appeared before me. The endless discussions about whether she was strong enough for this 'procedure'. The waiting: When would we have the result of the test that would tell us? Would the test be decisive? What did the test say? Should she have another test? What if we waited another twenty-four hours? Then the relief when a decision was made: Yes, they think her heart is strong enough.

One of the swing doors was pushed back for the woman in full theatre gear to put her head round.

'Nearly there,' she said. She screwed up her face in a kindly gesture of sympathetic pain. 'Sorry.'

The door closed with a bump. We were left to fill more time.

I looked down at the floor. What would I do if I was left on my own?

Dorothy had read my thoughts.

'Rescue work.'

I looked up.

'Do the rescue work. In memory of Elsa. And for the sake of all the other Elsas that need help.' She touched my hand. 'That's how you can give thanks for the fourteen years.'

Elsa... dear Elsa. She had come to me at eight weeks with a broken leg. From the time she recovered, she had made me get up and go and get some healthy exercise, she had helped keep my high blood pressure down and she had always been there with me. She was a German Shepherd dog and she had been the most perfect living thing.

When Elsa had gone the previous autumn I had not been able to face 'replacing' her and had spent lonely months missing her. A woman who did rescue work heard we had lost her and had rung. I told her it was too soon yet for me to have another dog. But she hadn't been ringing for me to adopt a dog of my own: Would I be a foster parent? She said because it was Christmas she had nine dogs in a garage. This was Cecilia and I discovered later it was really four. Though that was bad enough.

Dorothy and I were not professionals at dealing with dogs. Still, nine dogs in one garage... If we'd had some experience, like running a boarding kennels, then maybe we could have offered to help... But we'd not even had a difficult dog of our own; I'd taken Elsa to training classes just to keep her intelligent brain occupied. Cecilia said the big breeds needed special help; some of the rescue societies weren't keen on taking the guarding breeds such as German Shepherds. We could probably understand why, but then it's those guarding breeds that are more likely to fall into the hands of the wrong types who want them because of their image.

The swing doors opened and the woman in full theatre gear returned with the two men.

I leant over and said to Dorothy quickly, in a whisper, 'I will.'

She squeezed my hand and I thought she would break a bone. She gave me a huge smile and one of the men took the brake off. They started to wheel her away from me.

She looked round and said, 'I'll be back and we'll rescue the dogs together.'

Then the swing doors swallowed her up and she was gone.

A Special Day

Bang! Bang! Bang!

What was that? I thought.

The battery in the front door bell had long ago died on us and we didn't always hear somebody rapping on the door – but I couldn't fail to hear this, even though I was asleep.

Bang! Bang! BANG!

I looked at the clock: not yet eight o'clock. Whoever's banging on the front door at this time on a Sunday morning? In Little Wilberry?

It had taken Dorothy and me more than a year's house-hunting to find our cottage and its village. We had lived on a ring road in the city for years and felt we had earned a respite from the traffic. We longed for some peace, space, trees, fields, hedges, country lanes, wildlife. In the tiny East Anglian village of Little Wilberry and its countryside we had found all this.

The turning off the main road some three miles distant led only to our village and so we had no cars speeding through en route to somewhere more important. And the narrow, winding, patched-up road had made the village an unattractive prospect for developers. We still had five working farms in Little Wilberry, which gave some employment to a proportion of the village's small population. A handful of people worked away from the village, as I did, but many other residents were enjoying retirement.

This resident had been hoping to enjoy a Sunday morning lie-in.

Not fully awake, I pulled on trousers, found slippers, went downstairs and tugged at the front door, which was still sticking from the winter. Thankfully, the banging had stopped.

I pulled the door open to come face to face with a big, excited black dog up on his hind legs, pawing the air, almost filling the door frame. I stepped back.

At the other end of the black dog's lead was a man with his feet splayed out to give him grip, the end of the leather lead tightly wrapped around his hand.

The black dog dropped down onto all fours and lurched forward into the hall, pushing me aside, jerking his human after him. The man grabbed the doorpost with one hand and hung on, trying not to collide with me.

'You take in dogs?' he said.

'Um... We're probably *going* to take in dogs.' I thought, How does he know? Dorothy's still in hospital and we haven't decided yet.

'He's a lovely dog...' the man said.

The lovely dog turned sharp left behind me, his lead rubbing hard against the back of my legs. I think he wanted to explore our cottage.

'... but I can't keep him.'

It was raining, so I felt I ought to ask man and dog in. We went through to the kitchen. There the man wound his end of the lead twice more round his hand, to shorten it and get an even better grip.

'I'm sorry if I've disturbed you on a Sunday morning,' he said.

'It's OK,' I said.

'He's a lovely dog,' the man said again. 'But I can't keep him.'

The dog was pulling forward, straining at the end of the lead.

'Do you want to let him off?' I suggested.

'It's probably best if I hang on to him in here,' the man said.

Having just woken up, my mouth was dry. 'Would you like a cup of tea, or a coffee?' I asked.

'No. I'm fine, thank you.'

Well, I needed one badly so I took the kettle across to the sink to fill it. This gave me a little bit of time to gather my thoughts. I switched the kettle on and turned back to the man. I was about to explain that Dorothy and I had discussed embarking on rescue work with dogs, with a view to rehoming them, but hadn't yet finally decided as she was still in hospital. That if we did go ahead it wouldn't be until she was out of hospital and well on the road to recovery. But before I could say this the man held out his free arm to shake my hand.

'I'm John,' he said.

I shook his hand. 'I'm Barrie.'

'I know.'

I wanted to say, How do you know?

'I've rung about twenty places,' he said. 'No one will take him. I've used up three vouchers on me mobile.'

An awkward pause.

I looked across at the dog. He was so tall that his head was nearly level with the work surfaces in the kitchen. He was sniffing his way along them.

'Let him off,' I said.

John laughed what seemed to be a forced laugh. 'If you say so.'

He unclipped the lead and the dog immediately jumped up and put his feet on the work surface, sniffing the bread bin.

'Get down!' John shouted.

The dog ignored him. His owner grabbed the dog's collar and pulled him back down onto the floor.

'He's a devil for food,' he said. 'Never known a dog like him. Do anything for food.' He shook his head.

I noticed the dog's hip bones were protruding and his ribs showed. I recalled that our vet had once told us that you should be able to feel a dog's ribs, but not see them.

'Helps himself, does he?' I said.

'Oh, yes.' John chuckled nervously to himself.

I asked him if he wanted to sit down. He thanked me and sat down on a kitchen chair but didn't take his eye off the dog.

Neither of us spoke for a minute or two. While he watched what his dog was up to, I looked at John. It was difficult to estimate his age: thirties perhaps? He had wrinkles on a face that seemed too young to have deep wrinkles. He wore what I guess was a suit jacket, too long for him, over soiled jeans. In those moments of silence he began to rub his hands together as if he were washing them.

'He's enormous, isn't he?' I said, breaking the silence. 'How old is he?'

John chuckled to himself again, without looking up. 'Eleven months.'

'He's huge for eleven months,' I said.

'He's easy enough to handle, if you just remember he'll do anything for food.'

I was about to say that if Dorothy and I did decide that we would try the rehoming work – although it would be in our spare time – we might be able to take this dog in the not-too-distant future. I was about to say this when John looked up from watching the dog. Our eyes met.

'Don't change his name,' he said. Then he hesitated. Perhaps he thought that sounded as if he was presuming we would take the dog, which it did.

'I'm sorry,' I said, 'but...'

'When I was a squaddie my best pal was a dog handler. His dog Monty was shot. When I got this lad, I named him after him.' Now he looked away from me and down at the floor. He rubbed his forehead with the palm of his hand. 'It was in honour of him.'

The big, black dog went up to John, put his head against his arm and nudged him. John put out both his arms and cupped the dog's head in his hands.

'I'm sorry, lad,' he said. 'I'm sorry.'

I stood looking out of the window, looking down from high up in the tower block. It would soon be dusk and lights were starting to come on in buildings all over the hospital site. I compressed my lips. Imagine her having to be here today of all days.

I thought I heard footsteps in the corridor outside and turned quickly from the window, hoping it would be Dorothy.

Both beds in the little side-ward were empty. I pondered where Dorothy might be. Is she all right? There's nothing gone wrong? Then, knowing what she would say to me, I made the effort to say to myself, Don't panic, Mr Hawkins.

The door opened and there she was. Seeing me, she gave a great big smile. All these years and she can still curl my toes when she does that.

'Hello!' She said it with such warmth and enthusiasm.

Just two or three very long strides across the room and I had my arms around her, holding her tightly. 'I wondered where you were, I was beginning to wonder if everything was all right,' I said.

'I just wheeled Mrs Dawes, the lady in the other bed, down to the day room,' she explained.

'Oh, so we might have a bit of time to ourselves,' I said.

'And it gives her a change of scenery,' Dorothy said. Then gave me another big smile. 'And a chance for me to give you your present.'

'How can you have got me a present when you're in hospital?'

'Well, it is a bit of a limited choice in the hospital shop – but I had to get you *something*. I'll get you some proper presents when I come home.'

'I don't want anything – you coming home will be my present.' I'd put on a brave face up to then but now the bitterness and sadness came out. 'I can't believe you're in hospital today of all days. We should be together today. Not miles apart.'

'We're together *now* – enjoy this time. And I'll be coming home soon.'

'Yes. Yes, you will.'

'Don't you want your present?' she asked.

I nodded and then, having released some of the emotion I felt, was able to enjoy a small laugh. 'What is it? Don't tell me, a packet of Kleenex? Or a bag of grapes?'

She poked out her tongue. Then suddenly, 'Is that my card?' She had spotted something on her pillow.

She opened the pink envelope and took out the card. On the front of it a big white dog was sitting gazing down at a kitten. She sighed, smiled, and sat down on the bed to admire the picture.

I sat down beside her. 'I had a surprise this morning,' I said. 'Somebody knocked at the door at ten to eight and offered me a dog.'

She turned to look at me, nearly as surprised as I had been. 'No...'

'Some fella just turned up out of the blue. With an enormous black German Shepherd. Well, I think it's a Shepherd... '

She interrupted me. 'Oh, I wonder if it's Mrs Dawes' son. I told her we were thinking of doing some rescue work – I wonder if she told her son.'

'The bloke said his name was John.'

'Oh, I think she did say his name was John.'

'I told him we hadn't decided.'

'Did he tell you he was homeless?' Dorothy asked. 'She said her John was homeless.'

'Yes.'

'I'll ask her when she comes back. She didn't say too much but I gather he had some sort of a breakdown and he's been homeless for a while.'

She looked down at the dog on the card, gazing at it for some moments. Then, still looking at it, she said, 'I gather he was pretty desperate to find somewhere for his dog.' I watched as she rubbed a finger gently on the card as if she was stroking the dog in the picture.

I got up and went back to the window. Lights were on now in most of the windows across the hospital site. I could see my car in the car park below and had a sudden thought: Had I paid and displayed? I had had other things on my mind at the time.

'We might have taken him if I hadn't been in hospital,' Dorothy said. Then she added, trying to sound upbeat, 'He might still need help when I'm out of hospital and things have settled down.'

I was still looking out of the window. There were the sounds of footsteps and voices immediately outside the door. It seemed as if our little bit of space together was coming to an end. Without looking round from the window I said, 'I suppose you're not allowed outside yet.'

I looked round for the response and Dorothy shook her head.

I turned back to the window. 'It's just that I thought you might like to see him, that's all,' I said, trying to sound casual.

'See who?' Then her mouth dropped open and she took a deep breath. 'You've taken him...?'

I turned and nodded.

'Oh, Barrie!' She jumped up excitedly and ran across to me. 'While I was in hospital! Our first rescue!' She put her arms round me to give me a congratulatory hug. 'Where have you left him?'

'In the car.'

She took her head off my shoulder to look at me.

'That's why I asked if you could go outside – to meet him.'

She gazed at me for a few moments then turned to look out of the window. She stared down at the old Volvo estate parked below. It was still light enough to make out a big, black dog, curled up, in the back. Dorothy's eyes widened. She looked down at the Volvo and its occupant for several moments without speaking. Then she turned to me. 'Oh, Barrie... taking in our first orphan... what a wonderful thing to have done on our anniversary.'

She gazed at me, a smile on her face. Then the smile disappeared slowly. She furrowed her brow. 'Barrie... how will you cope?'

The question surprised me. 'We had a dog for fourteen years,' I replied. 'I do know a bit about it.'

'But what do you know about *this* dog? What problems has he got?'

I shook my head. 'Problems? I don't know.'

'Didn't you ask the chap?'

'No. I... I didn't think to.'

Dorothy managed an encouraging smile.

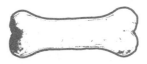

Food, Glorious Food

I looked back. And up. In the fading light I could see Dorothy at the window where I had stood. She waved and then blew me a kiss, but I turned away quickly in case she could see I was screwing up my face to stop myself from crying. In all the years we had been together this stay in hospital was the first time we had been apart.

As I approached the car I saw this big, black dog sitting in the back and had the cheering realisation that at least I would not be going home to an empty house tonight.

As he saw me coming, Monty stood up, but had to keep his head down; he was much too big for a Volvo estate. He gave a cautious wag of his tail. The thought occurred to me that he had been in the car quite a long time and I wondered if he needed to cock his leg. Visiting time at the hospital had ended and there were people coming to their cars. I hadn't thought to ask his owner what he was like with strangers, especially in fading light. The hospital was on the edge of the city and in just a couple of miles I would be out in the country. I knew of a lay-by where I could stop. A few minutes driving and I'd be there.

Sitting behind a tractor, however, an old tractor, a very slow tractor, along a winding country road, I began to hope that the boy in the back wasn't desperate.

I pulled into the lay-by at last with relief. Now nearly dark, I got out, went to the back of the estate to let the boy out and made a discovery: I needed a lead for him. I hadn't bothered to take a lead as we weren't going for a walk. I had just opened the back of the car and he had jumped in. John had said he loved cars; he wouldn't be the slightest bit of trouble in the car. And he'd been right.

Let him out here, in this lay-by, with no lead...? There wasn't anybody about, just a car parked at the other end of the lay-by. Still, I decided I wouldn't chance it. Then there was a *scratch... scratch... scratch* at the rear window. I looked at Monty. Was he asking to be let out? I wondered if he just wanted to get out because I had.

Scratch... scratch... SCRATCH! That last pawing at the window pulled the 'A Dog Is for Life' sticker off. Monty seemed tense – or was it my imagination?

Sudden inspiration: He loves food. John had said repeatedly, 'He'll do anything for grub.' In the car was a bag of grapes Dorothy had given me to take home; she had said nearly every visitor had brought her a bunch and she couldn't face looking at another grape for the rest of her life. I fetched the bunch out of the car. I would hold them behind my back, not let him see them until he'd done what he needed to and then I'd dangle them enticingly.

I opened the back. Monty looked at me, hesitating. I realised then I should have asked John what words of instruction he knew. What should I say to let him know he can get out?

I tried, 'OK.'

Success! Monty jumped down, looked around him, made straight for a nearby tree, then stopped to look at something that had caught his attention. He was gazing at the little car parked at the other end of the lay-by. He trotted off towards it.

'Monty!'

Monty quickened his pace.

'Monty!' If he was listening, this time he would have heard the anxiety in my voice.

He broke into a trot. I felt a rush of anxiety well up in my chest. I hurried after him, whipped the grapes round into view and dangled them at arm's length.

'Monty! Look – grapes!'

Monty was hurrying to the tiny car – whose passenger door was open. It was almost dark now and the car's interior light was on.

Monty got to the car, lowered his head and stuck it in. I started to run.

The front half of Monty disappeared into the car. I started to panic.

The back legs disappeared into the car, just his tail sticking out.

Running so fast now, I had a job to slow myself down and crashed into the car door. I ducked down to see inside the car. Monty blocked almost all the view, but I could see a very small man behind the wheel. He had slithered down his seat so far that his chin rested on his shoulders.

Monty's big, black head hovered above him.

Puzzlingly, the little man held his right hand up in the air, as if he was holding something, but there was nothing in it.

I stared at the scene. I didn't know what to say or do. The little man was also motionless, gazing up at Monty. Then he spoke. 'Good boy,' he said softly.

He turned his head, very slowly, to look at me.

'He ate my sausage roll,' he said.

I switched off the Volvo and took a deep breath. I was glad to be home after my adventure with Monty.

I turned round to look at him. He stood up – as best he could in a Volvo estate – and wagged his tail.

'You villain,' I said.

He wagged his tail faster and wider.

'Wait there until I get a lead.'

I wasn't going to let him out of that car without a lead a second time, in case there was somebody within a mile or two with a sausage roll.

Indoors, I looked round for the lead he had on when his owner brought him that morning. Had John taken it away with him? We had only been in the kitchen but it wasn't to be seen.

I did have a lead, Elsa's old one. I knew where it was of course, along with her bowl and her collar and her name-tag. Could I use it for another dog? My thoughts dwelt on that for several moments. I became aware of how quiet and still the house was.

Visions came back to me of dragging Monty by the collar out of the little man's tiny car and then, bent over, leading him back to the Volvo by his collar, then up and into the Volvo, still clinging on to the collar. I needed a dog lead.

I went into my study to get it and saw that the light was flashing on the answer machine. I switched on playback.

'Er... this is John – I brought you Monty. This morning. Look, I was too upset but there were some things I should have told you before I left. He's never—'

The message ended abruptly. A pause, then a second message came on.

'Hello, it's John again. I rang earlier – I ran out of credit. He's never lived in the house...'

So he's not house-trained, I thought.

'... so he's not house-trained. You can't let him sleep in the house. Oh, and he absolutely adores cheese – I think he'd do cartwheels for a bit of cheese. Give him my love, will you? Give him a great big hug for me, will you? Tell him I love him...'

The machine clicked off.

So where was Monty going to sleep? I pondered that little problem on my way back to the car, now armed with a lead. A dog that size that wasn't house-trained... The garage was the obvious thought – so don't let him out yet. We'll need a blanket or a duvet for him.

Where does Dorothy keep bedclothes? The top of the wardrobe proved wrong, as did the cupboard above the immersion heater. I didn't think to look in the drawers under the divan.

So what else could I use? I needed a new dressing gown – my old one had holes in the elbows – he could have that.

Walking up and down the garden, back and forth, Monty safely secured on Elsa's old lead, I had a new question to ponder about our first orphan: Would he cock his leg while on a lead? Up and down we went, then along the village street, then back again. A couple of times it was beginning to look hopeful... but nothing happened.

It was gone ten o'clock now and I'd had nothing to eat since lunchtime except for a few grapes. I led him into the garage, where I'd laid out his dressing gown and two breakfast bowls, one with water and one with some Big Value dog food John had left for him. Monty's eyes widened when he spotted the food and he dragged me towards it. He ate so fast it had gone by the time I unclipped his lead. I told him what a good boy he was and backed away towards the door. Would he try and follow me out? Would he try and bolt past me? No, he sat down on his haunches, and then slid down onto all fours. Clever dog – he knew what he was there for. I backed out of the side door of the garage and closed it with a sigh of relief. I needed some dinner, but what I needed even more was a cup of tea.

'Good night – I'll see you in the morning,' I called through the door.

I made for the house, feeling satisfied with a job well done and looking forward with happy anticipation to that cup of tea and a sit in my armchair.

Indoors, the kettle was soon on. I thought I could hear something above the noise of its boiling and switched it off to listen. No, all was quiet.

Then I heard it: *Howl! Howl! Howl!*

Through the silence that descended on our little village in the late, dark hours of a Sunday night, a large, black dog was howling: a soulful cry that would have been heard by our ancestors huddled around the campfire thousands of years ago. A cry that could send a cold chill down the spine of Wilberry residents, awakened from sleep, lying in their beds.

Then it stopped...

I stood motionless for several moments. Maybe it had just been his initial reaction to being left. Several more moments of silence, then: *Howl! Howl! Howl! Hooowl!*

I shut my eyes. This was a BIG problem. This was a very quiet village. The sort of place where some people go to bed at ten o'clock and if you stayed up to walk round the village at eleven o'clock there would hardly be a light on.

Howl! Hooowl! HOOOWL!

I marched out to the garage. 'No!' I shouted through the garage door. I was about to shout it again when I realised I was making as much noise as the dog. 'Be quiet, you naughty dog,' I hissed through the door. Within, all was silent. I waited for several long moments, ready with a stern voice if there was another outbreak.

Several minutes of peace and quiet passed. That's done the trick, I thought.

I made my way slowly back to the house – and that cup of tea. I strained to listen out over the noise of the boiling kettle, but outside all seemed quiet and still.

Tea was brewed. Many minutes had passed now and all was still peaceful in Wilberry. I stirred my tea – and dropped my spoon on the floor when I heard, *Howl! Howl! Howl! Howl! Howl!*

I was out the front door in a flash and racing to the garage. But what was I going to do?

Perhaps he just doesn't like the garage. Or, more worryingly, perhaps he's lonely?

Where else could I try for him? The chicken house? It's small, big enough only for four or five hens, but that may be a good thing; maybe he's used to a kennel. There's straw in it to make it cosy, and it's nice and clean and new. We'd bought it for chickens we were going to get when Dorothy came out of hospital.

Monty was delighted to see me when I reappeared and clipped Elsa's lead on again. He trotted happily down to the chicken house at the bottom of the garden.

I opened the door. 'In you go,' I said.

Monty looked round at the dark interior then down at the floor. He jerked his head back in surprise: presumably he'd never seen a straw floor.

'You'll be cosy in here,' I said.

I waved a hand to indicate for him to go forward. But Monty stayed outside, staring in.

Looking back now, I shake my head at some of the things I did in those early days. What would a dog trainer think of some of my techniques? Such as, on my own in the dark, with a dog that had met me only that day, a dog so big that when he stood up on his hind legs he was taller than me, standing behind him, trying to get him into a little chicken house, my hands on his hind quarters, shoving him from the rear?

But if Monty didn't want to go into that chicken house, then he wasn't going to go into that chicken house.

His owner's telephone message flashed into my mind: cheese!

Going back to the house, I rifled through the fridge for cheese. Would he prefer Cheshire or Gorgonzola?

I took chunks of both back to the chicken house and, deciding to try the Gorgonzola first – it smells more – waved a bit about in front of Monty.

'Hmmmm,' I said, holding it up to my nose and sniffing appreciatively. Monty's gaze was fixed on the cheese. I opened the door of the chicken house and threw the cheese to the far end. Monty leapt after it. In a flash I slammed the door behind him and slid the bolt across.

I crossed my fingers so hard it hurt, but this time I didn't even get back to the house. *Howl! Howl! Howl!*

Lights came on at one of the houses opposite. I looked at my watch: half past eleven. On a Sunday night. House-trained or not, he had to come in the house – it must be that he's lonely, I thought.

We trotted up to the house together, Monty's tail wagging as he enjoyed his moonlit outing. In our house there were deep pile carpets everywhere except the utility room. I laid down lots of newspaper on the floor. I looked at Monty – he is such a big dog – and put down more newspaper. The Cheese Trick worked again perfectly. I made a mental note to buy a big chunk the next day.

By this stage I realised I was exhausted. I'm going to bed, I thought.

Howl! Howl! Howl!

I froze and closed my eyes. I had run out of ideas. I put fingers in my ears. With eyes closed and fingers in ears, life became quite pleasant again. But I couldn't stand in the middle of the kitchen like that all night. As I opened my eyes and took my fingers out of my ears I heard the phone ringing.

I caught my breath. Could that be John? He said he might ring that night to see how Monty was. I made for the hall and grabbed the phone. 'Hello!'

'Hello, my Barrie.'

It was Dorothy! Oh, what a lovely surprise.

'I know it's late to ring you,' she said, 'but I didn't want to go to sleep without saying goodnight on our anniversary. I hope I didn't get you out of bed.'

'I wish,' I said, sighing.

'What's that noise?' she asked.

'That noise,' I said, 'is two rooms and two closed doors away – they must be able to hear it all along the street. I can't stop him howling, Dorothy.'

I went through it all with her. How I'd tried the garage, but he howled; how I'd tried the chicken house, but he howled; how I'd tried the utility room, but he howled.

'I wish you were here,' I said. 'I don't know what to do.'

I was sunk in gloom and at my wits' end.

'He didn't howl when you had him in the car,' Dorothy said.

'Erm... no.'

'Well, put him in the car.'

'Let him sleep in the car...?'

'He's probably used to it. John's homeless.'

I shrugged my shoulders. I had given up hope. 'I'll try,' I said.

Monty bounded out of the utility room. He looked up at me expectantly. No, I thought, not yet. Cheese is only for when I want you to go in somewhere you don't want to go. I opened the back of the Volvo. Monty jumped in before I even got the cheese out of my pocket.

'Goodnight, for the fourth time,' I said.

I didn't bother to make for my armchair. I waited behind the front door. The car was on the drive at the front of the cottage, the closest yet to the neighbours, so I wanted to be able to get out there as fast as I could.

While waiting for Monty to start, I thought about the day's events. About how, unplanned, we'd taken in our first orphan. That in doing so the decision to start the rescue work had been made for us. And how hard it would have been to turn the dog away, how hard it would have been to say no to his owner, who was so desperate for help, for somewhere for his dog to go. And how useless I'd been in handling the dog. I'd taken him off out without even a lead. I thought about the reckless way I'd carried on, pushing at the backside of this huge dog who'd only known me for a few hours and could have made shredded Barrie of me.

And then I realised something else: all was quiet.

Hardly daring to breathe, tiptoeing as lightly as I possibly could on the gravelled drive, I inched my way to the Volvo. Close to, I could hear a noise, a sort of rumbling sound. At first I thought it was my tummy. I leant over to see in the back of the car – and then I knew what the sound was.

It was the sound of snoring.

A Quick Start

I woke up suddenly and looked at the clock: ten to five. Ten to five? Why was I awake at five o'clock in the morning? Then I remembered. Today was the day Dorothy was coming home from hospital. In my sleep I must have been wishing away the night, wanting it to be morning. Another week had passed since our anniversary and I ached to have her back with me, safe and well.

I lay there for what seemed ages, trying to get back to sleep. What's the time now? Ten *past* five? Only twenty minutes later? Might as well get up and start clearing up the house. There isn't a clean plate left.

One minute past nine and the phone was ringing. Unusually, I was pleased to hear it, as Dorothy had said she would ring to let me know what time she would be let out, for me to be her chauffeur home. I grabbed the phone.

'Hello.'

'Mr Hawkins?'

'Er, yes.' It wasn't Dorothy. The caller couldn't have failed to pick up the tone of disappointment in my voice.

'I believe you help people who can no longer keep their dog?'

If this woman had been present she would have seen me standing with my mouth open. How did she know this? It was incredible how word had spread. We had only mentioned it to a few people we knew.

The silence was interrupted not by the caller but by Monty.

Crash!

I knew immediately what that was.

'Excuse me one moment,' I said into the phone, and made straight for the kitchen.

I pushed the door open and trod in something soft. My foot started to slide and I grabbed the door. The previous evening I had slid on some mouldy tinned tomatoes I had found at the back of the fridge, there from before Dorothy had gone into hospital, which had been retrieved from the bin by Monty. That time I had slid and bumped against a stack of dirty dishes on the cooker, sending them crashing onto the washing machine. This time I did better and held on to something.

I had already learnt not to eat in the same room as Monty. On his second day with us I was eating microwave chips and veggie sausages on my lap in front of the telly. While I watched the telly, Monty watched me. Sitting on his haunches, his gaze followed every forkful from plate to mouth.

Hearing a noise outside, I looked round to the living room window and listened out intently. A friend had said he might call round that night to cheer me up and I hoped it was him, but all was quiet. I turned back to my sausage and chips, but something was wrong – it was just chips. I gazed at the plate, empty on one side. I was sure there had been a sausage left.

And where was Monty? I leaned over the arm of the chair to look round the room. There, under the table, half-hidden by a tablecloth, I could see an enormous black dog, silently licking his lips. How could a dog that big have removed a sausage from my plate, on my lap, carried it to the other side of the room, got under the table and eaten it, all without my hearing or seeing a thing?

'You villain!' I said.

This was Orphan Dog Number One, and I was learning. I was learning that when you took in somebody else's dog you took in any bad habits he had been allowed to develop.

Today's squelchy mess on the floor was strawberry trifle. I really mustn't leave anything on the worktop if Monty is in the kitchen. I tutted to myself. I'd have to clear this mess up when I finished on the phone. Monty sat on his haunches, waiting to be told off, by the look on his face. The yellow blob on the end of his nose would have made for a good photo.

I went back to the phone.

'Sorry about that,' I said.

'My name is Sarah Phipps and I have a dog that is two years old and—'

I had to stop her before she went on.

'I'm sorry but we've only just started this—'

'Pearl's a very easy dog – she's not got any problems – that's not why I'm trying to home her.'

'No, I'm sure. What I meant was that we aren't set up properly. If we're going to do this on any scale we're going to have to build kennels and runs in the garden.'

'She could live in the house. She's always lived indoors.'

'I've already taken in one that's living in the house.' I looked in the direction of the kitchen. 'And it's not turning out to be easy.'

'She's my best friend – it's not that I want to get rid of her.'

There were several moments' silence. I wanted to help, of course, but I'd already taken in a dog before we had planned to get started. Dorothy couldn't come out of hospital to share the house with two strange dogs. Take in somebody else's adult dog and it's not used to you, it's not used to doing what you ask, it doesn't know your routine, it's likely to be unsettled, restless, missing its previous owner – it might even be howling!

'I have terminal cancer, Mr Hawkins,' the woman said.

Now it was my turn to fall silent. It was an uncomfortable silence – I didn't know what to say. But I had to say something.

'I'm sorry,' was all I could think of.

'I have to go into hospital this week. I have rung so many places and nobody will take my dog.'

This was something I was going to hear many, many times in the future.

'I'm not afraid to die, Mr Hawkins. I'm just afraid of what will happen to my dog when I do.'

For an awkward moment I said nothing and gazed into space, stunned.

Then I found myself saying, quietly, 'We'll take Pearl and we'll look after her. And we'll find her a lovely home. And she will be fine.'

And that's how it was that when Dorothy left hospital – after all those weeks, after that six-hour operation – she returned to find that she was to share her home with *two* new residents who had moved in while she had been away.

How different they were: Monty pure black, Pearl pure white. And the contrast in their colour was reflected in their characters. Monty was a bruiser, Pearl soft and gentle. Monty was always rushing about, while Pearl would lie with her head resting on her paws, watching us. With Monty we were always wondering, What's he up to now? Pearl just dropped in to our routine, as if she had always been with us.

Of course with Dorothy convalescing it wasn't the right time to be taking a strange dog into our home, let alone two. Two dogs to walk, feed and generally look after.

The first dog my wife had known about, the second caused her to stare open-mouthed in the hallway when we got back from hospital. She could see a white dog through the frosted glass in the kitchen door; she had been expecting to see a black one.

'What...? Barrie...? What...?'

I had some explaining to do.

I just said that I had to take Pearl, as a way to give thanks. Because the most important person in Pearl's life would not come out of hospital and the most important one in mine had.

Healthy Exercise

'Oooooooowwww! Aaaaaww! Huurrr!'

It was so unexpected. So sudden. So *painful.*

I was enjoying a walk along the country track, the evening sun on the back of my neck, appreciating the quiet and green of the countryside, at peace with the world, then something careered into me from behind, at the speed of an InterCity Express. It hit me in the back of my legs, knocking me right up into the air then down onto my back with such a thud I was gasping for breath. For several moments I just did not know what had happened to me. It *felt* like a train crash. Forty-five kilos of bone and muscle hurtling into me, the collision made my top and bottom teeth clang together.

'You mad dog!' I managed to call out, even though I was fighting to get my breath.

It was my first walk with Monty off the lead. I had been apprehensive about undertaking it but it was my arms that compelled me to try. We had had him over a week now and my arms had grown a little longer every day. It wasn't just that he pulled on the lead; it was that he progressed on the lead in a manner

Dorothy came to call 'helicoptering'. Like the blades of a helicopter, Monty would whirl round, with me in the centre. I had a choice: either I could end up with the lead wrapped round me several times, so I couldn't move, or I had to spin round with him. After a few spins I would get giddy. On one of our walks I fell in a hedge.

But the worst aspect of walking him on a lead was the birds. It was all right if they didn't move, but see Monty coming and what did they do? They flew off, and then I would fly off as Monty took off after them. I'd lost count of how many times it felt like he had jerked my arm out of its socket. I would spend half the walk rubbing the top of my arm and my shoulder and within the first week had used up the whole tube of ointment for muscle pain I found in the medicine drawer.

Then there was his inquisitiveness. Many of the houses in the village had a wall low enough for Monty to look over, or a picket-type fence he could peer through. But one neat, detached bungalow had a wall too high for him to see over. On our first walk Monty felt it was necessary to jump up, rest his paws on the top of the wall and get a clear view of the immaculate garden. The occupant must have been bending over the flower border exactly at the spot where Monty's big head appeared. This elderly gentleman straightened up to find himself up close, face to face with Monty, took a couple of steps backwards and toppled over. After that, we always walked a different route.

Rubbing the backs of my knees now, I wished I hadn't used up all of that tube of ointment on my arms.

'You mad dog,' I said again, 'I could murder you!' Monty didn't look worried; he wagged his tail. I sat for several minutes rubbing the backs of my knees, my bottom, my elbows, my head. The crash had shaken me up and given me a headache.

Monty wandered off to investigate more interesting things than me but came back when I didn't get up. He stood looking at me, then tilted his head sideways as if puzzled.

'First you frighten the life out of me, then you break both of my legs!'

It was an exaggeration, of course, to accuse him of breaking my legs; it just felt like it. But it isn't an exaggeration to say he had frightened the life out of me at the start of the walk.

I had needed somewhere quiet to walk him, where we wouldn't meet people. On our lead walks in the village, if he saw a person he would want to rush up to them, towing me along behind. It wasn't that he was a threat to them, it was his inquisitiveness. He wanted to investigate them. Dorothy said it was another sign of his intelligence. No doubt she was right, but I also thought a huge black dog rushing up to people was a way to alarm them. So I had driven out to Hope Hill, where we had walked sometimes in the past with our Elsa. It was a few miles from the nearest village and we had only ever met a tractor there.

The countryside surrounding Wilberry was criss-crossed by a network of tracks used by farm vehicles and some walkers. These numerous tracks were the by-product of how farmers in the area held their land. Instead of the land making one continuous holding adjacent to the farmhouse, it was common for a farmer to have fields scattered throughout the locality. Because of the need to reach their fields, there were more tracks, or 'droves' as they were called, than might be found in other rural areas. This was a discovery Dorothy and I made after moving to the village and was a feature of the local countryside for which we were to become grateful, especially after we commenced the rescue work. In the city, street after street of tarmac and pavement had been broken up by the occasional park. Here we were surrounded by hundreds of acres of green countryside and the droves gave us access to it and miles of walks.

I had let Monty out of the Volvo, feeling fairly confident he wasn't going to run off, that he would come back to me when called. I was now the Cheese Man. In the garden I only had to pat my left trouser pocket and he would come rushing up. That was the pocket I kept the bag in, the one with the cheese cut up by Dorothy into little cubes.

The drove I planned to walk was halfway up a rise, an area of the local countryside where there were small fields marked out by hedges and trees. We had gone perhaps only a couple of hundred yards before I felt the need to stop and appreciate what was around me, the differing shades of green, of brown, of gold. Colours that calmed me.

I had the presence of mind to think, Enjoy this, Barrie, but keep an eye on Monty. I looked around. He was a few yards behind me, motionless like a statue, his head lowered, gazing at a toad. My movement may have alarmed the toad, for he hopped off to disappear in the grass verge. Monty looked up at me and I smiled back at him. We think we are alone, but of course we are surrounded by small creatures, including some we never see.

I turned back to savour the picturesque scene. It was spring; I had the rest of springtime and all of the summer to look forward to and enjoy. I took a few slow deep breaths and realised then how peaceful it was. A sense of calm well-being came over me.

It was interrupted by the thought, Barrie, keep an eye on Monty. I looked behind me again, casually. No Monty to be seen. I swivelled my head all around, this time concentrating. Was that him in that field, or was it something else? The something else didn't move. I scanned further. I wasn't feeling relaxed now. I put my hand to my forehead to shield my eyes from the sun and scanned the horizon.

Where was he? I knew I shouldn't have taken my eyes off him!

'Monty!' I called out. Then louder: 'Monty!' I spun round to call in the other direction. 'MONTY! COME!'

I was alone. Why would he run off? In the garden if I called he would always come immediately – he must have been so far away already he couldn't hear me. It had taken me half a minute to go from serenity to panic.

My chest started to rise and fall with anxiety. I wished Dorothy was with me. I'd have to go home and get her – I couldn't find him on my own out there. What was I going to do?

'Monty! Monty! M-O-O-O-O-ONTY!'

All was still and silent.

But only for a few moments – because then I heard it. A rumbling like distant thunder. I looked in wonder at the clear blue sky stretching to the horizon.

The noise was getting louder and closer. I turned in the direction it was coming from. It was getting louder still. Whatever was making that noise? It was coming from the grass field that went up the horizon. I realised it was coming from over the ridge, from something out of sight.

Then, in this isolated and formerly tranquil area of English countryside – and I am prepared to testify to this on oath in a court of law – I felt the ground begin to tremble. It dawned on me where I had heard the noise before: on the telly. In Westerns. When the herd stampeded.

Over the ridge came a big, black dog, ears back, tail between his legs, running for his life.

Seconds later the herd followed: a big herd of cattle thundering towards... me. And I was separated from them by two strands of wire purporting to be a fence.

More and more of them came into view. Some of them had horns. Some of them had very big horns. Some of them were wide-eyed. Now Monty was just a few yards away. He ducked under the wire and shot past me.

I spun round and ran, feeling a tightening in my chest. How could that silly little fence hold that galloping herd? My short legs carried me along faster than they ever had before. I covered two or three hundred yards in seconds, inspired by sprinters I'd seen on the telly and by fear, face screwed up with the agony of effort.

On the other side of the track there was a ditch – should I jump it? Was the sound of the thundering hooves subsiding? Had the fence held them? I dared to twist my head and look back. The beasts were turning away before getting to the fence. Force of habit? I closed my eyes in relief then promptly opened them again – remember the ditch!

I slowed and stopped and collapsed against a tree, drained by running and terror. Monty lay down beside me, with his great tongue hanging out the side of his mouth, panting. What had he done to get the herd in such a state? Then I noticed the little figures at the back of the herd and I recalled reading how protective a cow could be of her calf. I had another thought: a German Shepherd is a sheepdog. I looked down at Monty. 'Had you been trying to round them up? Is that it, you barmy dog?' His tail brushed backwards and forwards across the grass.

Shaking my head now at the thought of this earlier near-miss, I took a break from rubbing my knees. I sat there on the ground, looking up at this big dog. It was the first time I had really paused to study him. He had those big pointed ears, the trademark of the German Shepherd. But he had not been painted the classic black and tan of his breed. Monty was an uncommon pure black. His former master, John, must have regularly brushed him for Monty's black coat shone. He had been running – he was always running – and his tongue was lolling out of the side of his mouth, which even now is the longest tongue I have seen.

'You were two hundred yards *ahead* of me when I last saw you,' I said to him, 'and then you've rushed at me from behind!' I shook my head. 'I know you've got loads of energy – I expect a dog your age to run about – but anyone would think you've got a firework up your bum! And if you *are* going to rush about as if you're demented, why don't you look where you're going?'

During the few days he had been with me, whenever he committed a misdemeanour – such as the incident of the vanishing sausage – to vent my feelings I had told him he was a villain. In the future Dorothy was to prove herself far better than me in assessing the character of the orphans who were to come to us, and she had showed it first with Orphan Number One.

'He's not a villain, not a deliberate wrong-doer,' she had said. 'He's growing up, and he's got to the stage where he's finding his feet, beginning to feel confident, beginning to feel he can throw his weight about – but he's still immature, not good at making judgements.'

Monty was gazing at me with his hazel eyes.

'I know what you are then,' I said, and put my hand on his head to stroke him. 'You're a teenager!'

His tail brushed back and forth across the grass again.

I rubbed the backs of my knees. 'But I like you,' I added. And then began gently stroking his head.

The day would come when I was to find out just how much I liked Orphan Number One.

Doubt

Road after road after road after road, and all looked the same. Called a 'new town' when it was built after World War Two, it seemed never-ending to me, now a village yokel. It had taken just sixty minutes from home to this place, but I was in a different world.

As I tried to understand the map I had drawn I wished I had taken more care over it. The woman on the phone had given me detailed directions; I guessed now that she was used to doing so for anyone trying to find her house. I had drawn my 'map' on the back of a magazine that had been lying by the phone – we really must, I now decided, if we are to do this rescue work, keep a notepad and pen by the phone at all times. I couldn't even read some of my own writing. What did 'bapo' mean? The circles were obviously roundabouts, but how about what seemed to be a little stick person wearing a large hat? Now I was paying the price for my sloppiness: late and lost.

This was a new experience, something I hadn't contemplated when making that decision to take in and find homes for dogs, that some of those dogs would have to be collected. I had agreed to take the woman's dog and it was only then she had told me she couldn't bring it. She didn't have a car. No, she hadn't got a relative she could ask. No, she couldn't ask a friend either: they all had kids they couldn't leave. So we had had to send a chauffeur to pick up our third orphan – and I was the chauffeur.

Where was I?

I needed a helpful person to ask for directions, but considering there were all these houses I had seen remarkably few human beings. I drove slowly, looking left and right for Barnes Road South, a name on my map that was legible. A trio of young males sitting on a wall, seemingly doing nothing, gave me a challenging stare. I decided I wouldn't bother them. Another half a dozen side roads and an elderly gentleman, picking up litter that had blown into his garden, looked more promising. He took time and care with his directions. Now I understood what some of my scribbled words said and what my symbols stood for, although the little stick person with the big hat remained a mystery. I told the elderly man I was really grateful. And I was.

The initials 'CDS' on my map turned out to be my abbreviation for cul-de-sac. The road was narrow; on either side cars were parked half on the pavement. Number 43 was in the corner. The woman on the phone had warned me not to park next door or her neighbour would come out and put a nasty note on my car – but which 'next door' did she mean? I parked outside 43, taking great care not to protrude into the roadway on either side.

So this was where the dog lived. The grass at the front and side was about a foot high, some children's toys were scattered about here and there and a rusting tumble dryer lay on its back, dead. Banging the door-knocker instantly set off excited barking somewhere inside the house. If that was the dog I had come for then he had a loud, deep bark. I waited for what seemed to be more than enough time for somebody to answer then knocked harder, although if there was anybody at home surely that barking would have told them someone was about? I was wondering if the dog's owner had given up waiting for me and gone out when a woman appeared from round the side of the house.

'Hello,' I said.

'You're the dog man?' the woman said.

'Er... I guess I am.'

'He's in the kitchen, so I'll let you in the front.' She turned and disappeared back round the side of the house.

Another wait until the front door was opened. On entering the house an unpleasant smell immediately hit me. The woman led me into the living room, picked up a packet of cigarettes and took one out.

'You must be Mrs Jackman,' I said.

'*Ms* Jackman,' she corrected.

Two children, under-fives I would guess, appeared from the hallway. I could see the curiosity in their faces: they had come to see the caller.

'I told you to keep out,' Ms Jackman said. 'Get out!' The girl turned and went out, but the boy stayed where he was.

Ms Jackman turned back to me. 'Do you want to sit down?'

I dropped down onto a low three-seater settee. I noticed the excited barking had become more excited.

Ms Jackman found a lighter on the mantel and lit her cigarette. 'As I said on the phone, I've only had him three weeks.' She blew a big ball of smoke into the air. 'I can't cope with him. He's too strong.'

'Right,' I said, to show I understood her situation.

Ms Jackman went out and stood in the hallway. 'Shut up!' she shouted. The barking stopped. She came back into the room. 'I've got three little-uns and you can't push a pushchair and keep hold of two of them and hold him at the same time. I can't take him out.'

'How did you get him?'

'I was in the pub!' She said this with a tone of 'Would you believe it?'

'We was at a table and a bloke at the bar just turned round and said, "Anybody want a dog?" I've always liked Alsatians and I've always wanted one, although he's not a true Alsatian. He's crossed with a Husky, the bloke said. He's such a powerful dog.'

'He must be,' I said. I assumed it was him that had resumed barking.

'I'll let him in,' Ms Jackman said. 'I warn you, he barks, but he's all right.'

'What's his name?' I asked.

'Claude. It's a stupid name.'

She went out into the hall followed by the boy. I could make out the sound of a door opening, then the sound of running paws.

The dog rushed in then, seeing me, braked suddenly. Coming to a halt in the middle of the room, he jerked his head back as if he had been taken by surprise. At the sight of me he set off barking furiously. He stood feet astride, eyes widened, staring at me. *Bark – bark – bark – bark – bark – bark!*

I did not know what to do. Where was the woman?

This was aggressive barking. I felt queasy in my tummy. I took a deep swallow. Looking straight back at the dog could be taken as a challenge, but I dare not take my eyes off him in case he suddenly came forward. He was just three or four feet away from where I sat on the low settee.

He was black and tan but mostly black with a dark face. Opening his jaws to bark showed off all his white teeth, level with my face.

With ferocious barking just feet away, the natural reaction is to back off: I pushed myself deeper into the settee. The movement caused the dog to spring forward. He curled his lips and snapped his jaws. He was so close I could touch him. He projected his head forward – I slipped further down in the seat. This made him more excited, more agitated. His head was above mine, inches from my face.

I felt sick.

'STOP IT!'

I was so tense that the sudden shout made me jump. But I still dared not take my eyes off the dog. Ms Jackman came into my line of sight, raised her hand and whacked him across the rump.

To no avail. She stepped forward, grabbed his collar and dragged him away. He was still barking and looking at me as he was dragged across the room.

'Now sit down! Stop it!' Ms Jackman shouted.

He didn't sit, but he did stop barking. She was standing in front of him and he moved his head so he could see round her and keep an eye on me. Still clutching his collar, Ms Jackman sat down and stubbed out her cigarette. The dog set off barking again but this time not with such force, more a reminder, I felt, to let me know he was still there. This was the guarding breed in him, the German Shepherd in him.

With her free hand Ms Jackman slapped him sharply on the nose. He shut his eyes and jerked his head back. It made me wince. During the fourteen years we had our German Shepherd, Elsa, never had I hit her. At the training class I had taken Elsa to as a youngster the experienced trainer had told me, 'Never smack your dog across the nose.' And his compelling reasoning had stayed in my memory. 'Your hand should be a source of comfort to your dog, not used to hit him. Otherwise, when he sees your hand coming, how is he to know whether it is to stroke him or to strike him?'

Claude gave one more bark, a soft one. It was as if he couldn't resist it. A cuff across the head this time. I looked away.

'I've left me ciggies in the kitchen,' Ms Jackman said. She got up and, leaning over to keep hold of the dog's collar, she walked him out of the room.

I stared at the carpet. This dog had frightened me, really frightened me. Could I take him?

Then again, could I leave him?

I stood outside the back door looking down our long garden. Beyond the hedge at the bottom of the garden was what, before we moved in, had been the vegetable garden. Now it was a wilderness of weeds. Beyond that was formerly a paddock: now a jungle of grass and wild growth up to the chest. And beyond that was the old barn with its new occupant. Not that I could see either the ex-vegetable garden or the ex-paddock in the dark. Nor the old barn, my destination.

The church clock struck eleven. I stood in the darkness, thinking. In one hand I held a dog bowl, in the other a small torch.

Ms Jackman had telephoned three times in the past week asking me to take Claude. During the final phone call she had introduced a threat: 'I don't want to but if no one will take him off me I'll have to take him to the vet.'

An empty threat? How was I to know?

With two orphans already living in the house with us, Monty and Pearl, it had been obvious to Dorothy and me that if we were to take a third we would need somewhere to keep him.

We had needed a quick – and cheap – solution. Dorothy came up with the idea of making use of a corner of the old barn. Some wood and some wire would make a temporary pen, although it never entered our heads that I should do the work. We had learned many years previously that it was not sensible for me to attempt carpentry. I had spent four hours one Saturday putting up a shelf which had later, in the middle of the night, crashed to the floor, taking a vase and flowers with it. Somebody in the village knew somebody who could do the work in the barn for us.

I had been surprised when he knocked at the door to say he'd finished already, but then, on inspection, it wasn't as sturdy as I had hoped for. I certainly had doubts about the wire. When I had said 'wire' I had had something stronger in mind than chicken wire to hold a German Shepherd/Husky.

As I stood at the back door, gazing down the garden towards the old barn in the blackness beyond, scenes from earlier that day came back to me: the dog rushing into the room at the woman's house, barking at me with excited ferocity; and barking in my face, four or five inches away; the nerve-wracking journey home. I hadn't yet learned that for a rescue dog's safety he or she needed to be secured in the car with a lead. There is plenty of room in the back of a Volvo estate, but it's dangerous for a dog and a distraction for the driver for the dog to be leaping about. Then when you get home and lift the tailgate, somehow you've got to stop the dog jumping out and running off. Thank goodness, when I got home Dorothy, the problem-solver, was waiting. She let Claude out of the passenger door, where it was easier to catch hold of him.

'I knew I should have come with you,' she had said, when I recounted my stomach-tightening meeting with the dog. But I wouldn't let her. She had not been home from hospital long and was supposed to be convalescing, regaining her strength, not doing anything that could put at risk the forty stitches. Her consultant had taken me aside to warn me, 'You must avoid situations that are stressful for Dorothy.'

That was why I would not let her come down with me now to the old barn.

Could I do this? I stared down the garden at the blackness beyond the few feet of light thrown out from the kitchen window.

The moon and stars were hidden by dark clouds that night. I had to go down to the old barn into that blackness armed only with a little torch – why hadn't I thought to buy a big, powerful lantern-type thing?

As I stood there, I realised we had taken the decision to go into rescue work too lightly. We had been drawn into it with thoughts of helping dogs that needed us, of putting our spare time to good purpose, of putting something back for all the pleasure and benefit we'd had from the fourteen years with our Elsa. And for me there had been some element of 'doing good deeds' and the need to become a 'better person'.

But now, staring down the garden into that blackness, reality was beginning to set in. It's not as if we were going to be tangling with little breeds of dog that probably couldn't do much harm to us.

I reminded myself why, for more than any other reason, I had wanted to do this work. We had taken in only three dogs so far, and yet in each case the owners had almost given up hope of finding somewhere to place these dogs, each a member of a guarding breed.

But then, if some other dog rescue organisations were wary of taking in the guarding breeds, who could blame them? Who wanted to go through what I had gone through that afternoon? Most sanctuaries most of the time are offered far more dogs than they can take. Why not take in the friendly, tail-wagging little spaniel, so much easier to home?

That dog down in the barn had only met me once. and that was in daylight. Now I was going to come walking out of the darkness. Why should he let me put him on a lead and take him round the garden? Who was I? Where had he been brought to? Would I hit him on his nose?

He was probably frightened by the unfamiliar noises in the spooky old barn: the creaking, the loose corrugated panel banging in the wind, the flapping birds in the roof. I know I was. And I'm afraid of the dark, always have been. I clutched my little torch.

I had chosen to do this work and down in that barn now was a dog I had taken in to help, confined in a pen, needing food and water and to come out for some exercise and to relieve himself.

I could do it. This time. Because he was there. I had to. But did I really want to put myself through this again with more dogs?

'I'm coming, Claude,' I said to the night air.

Helping with Enquiries

The phone was ringing.

We were only a few weeks into our rescue work and yet the phone rang already far more than before. And it was incredible how often it rang just as I picked up my knife and fork.

I sighed, put them down again, went out into the hall and snatched up the phone.

'Hello.' The tone of annoyance would have been obvious to any caller.

'Oh, hi,' said a friendly voice. 'Are you the guy with the sanctuary for dogs?'

Sanctuary for dogs? I hadn't thought of it like that. It was my house.

'Erm... well, we do take in dogs, but—'

'I hope you can help me. I'm getting desperate. I got a letter from the local authorities and now I've got your police on my tail. And I've got the military police onto me as well. I do not want the police on my tail. Sir, I do not.'

My caller was obviously with the American air-force base in the next county. Some of the personnel lived in houses in our area, rented out to the US authorities.

One of the houses in Wilberry had been occupied by a succession of American families over the years; the couple currently living there had often stopped to speak to us, to admire Elsa when we were out walking.

'I'm really hoping you can help me, sir,' my caller added.

I sighed. Three weeks and I already had three dogs. But weren't they adorable. Momentarily I pictured them in my mind: Monty, Pearl and Claude. It brought a smile to my face.

'It's certainly getting urgent, sir.'

But where would I put the dog?

'The letter from your local authorities says they'll bring me up on charges before your court if I don't control them.'

Them?

'Did you say "them"?'

'Oh yeah – a boy and a girl. Brother and sister. I think that's why I'm finding it so hard to get someone to take them on. But you know I'd hate to split them up. They've been together since they were little pups.'

Brother and sister? I paused. 'Well... if you'd like to give me your phone number, I'll see what I can do...'

I told Dorothy about the brother and sister. And that there was a danger of them being split up. But where would we put them? We already had two in the house, Monty and Pearl, and Claude in the barn, in theory at least, as he was spending more and more time in the house. He loved to be with people. He'd been wary that first night I had gone down to the barn but his need for company had won. Now he liked to lie across my feet. I could believe he was a Husky cross: he was thickset and heavy.

Boarding kennels seemed the only answer for these two siblings. But that would cost hundreds of pounds a month in fees. The night I had gone down to Claude in the old barn for the first time, the safety implications of what we had embarked upon had hit me. Now I was beginning to realise the financial implications. Pearl, the gentle, white female had come to us with a vaccination card, but I noted that the annual booster was due next week. That would be the start of the vet bills.

'And we need to be thinking about how we are going to find new homes for the dogs,' Dorothy said. Good point. 'We're not going to be like the big rescue societies with pens full of dogs, where people can come and have a look round on a Sunday afternoon.'

I couldn't help but reflect on how, by just telling a few people what we were going to do, the phone had been ringing with offers of dogs, but it hadn't been ringing with any offers of a home.

'What do people do who've got a litter to find homes for?' Dorothy pondered. Good point. They advertise them. I had a sudden thought: there was often an advert on the board in the village shop. Not our village shop – that, sadly, had closed many years ago – we had to use the store at a big village nearby. In among the postcard adverts on their board there were often pups for sale.

I would go and put a card up in Great Fosfen the next day, Friday, so it would be in for the weekend, when the shop was usually at its busiest.

I was an early customer on the Friday morning. The girl behind the till placed my card on a shelf. I wanted to get our campaign to find homes launched so I offered to pin it up on the board for her. As I left the shop, out of the corner of my eye I saw an elderly woman had stopped to run her eye over the board.

Back home, as I opened the front door, the phone was ringing.

'Hello,' I said in an unusually enthusiastic tone, hoping for good news.

Yes, the caller was replying to our advert!

So much of what we were doing was new to us and we were having to find our way as we kept coming up against questions we had to answer. One such question had been, Should we advertise that we had a number of dogs for rehoming, or should we advertise just one particular dog?

Dorothy had said, 'Let's concentrate on just one at a time. Let's rehome that dog as well as we possibly can. We're lucky, not being one of the big, national animal welfare societies with hundreds of dogs to rehome. We can give the dogs that come to us a Rolls-Royce rehoming service.'

So this telephone call was the very first call to our Rolls-Royce service, offering a home to one of our orphans.

'Do you still have the dog?'

'We do,' I replied.

'Does your dog bark?' the man asked.

The first dog we were trying to find a home for was of course our Orphan Number One, Monty.

'Oh yes,' I replied. And I could have added, 'And he also howls,' but I didn't mention that at this stage.

'Do you do part-exchange?'

I paused.

'I beg your pardon?' I said.

'My dog don't bark. I got him to guard me yard. If yours barks I'll give you mine and a tenner for it.'

The phone was ringing again.

I eyed it warily. The quality of that first call had been a shock. But then I reflected that life was like that: the very first call in response to our advertisement would have to be from a lunatic. Having got him out of the way, the rest of the calls would be from normal people.

I picked up the phone. 'Hello.'

'Mr Hawkins?' It was a formal tone of voice.

'Yes.' I furrowed my brow. I didn't put my name in the advert, did I?

'This is PC Morecambe speaking.'

The police? What do they want?

My brow furrowed again. I had read at some time that the pulse rate of even completely innocent citizens quickens when they are questioned by the police. I was such a citizen.

The officer coughed into the phone. 'Excuse me,' he said, then coughed several more times. He didn't sound a very healthy policeman. I wished he would get on with what he had to say.

'I understand you have a German Shepherd dog you want to rehome.'

Oh, so he has seen the advertisement! But no, he can't have done because he knows my name and my name wasn't in it...

A couple more coughs at the other end of the phone. 'I'm a police dog handler. I'm looking for a youngster I can train up.'

Really? Is this how the police get their dogs? I had always assumed police dogs were specially bred for the purpose.

'My vet, Melissa Gee, tells me you've recently gone in for rescuing dogs, German Shepherds in particular. That's a very worthwhile thing to do.'

So that was how he knew my name. Melissa was our vet as well. But this phone call immediately threw up yet more questions that Dorothy and I had not contemplated. When we had talked about finding homes we had only thought about homing the dogs as family pets. Would we be happy to home them as working dogs? With organisations? More questions immediately jumped into my brain: How would the dogs be treated? Did they stay with just the one handler? What happened when they were too old to go on working?

It seemed this dog handler was accustomed to dealing with such concerns raised by current owners. Before I had time to ask any of the questions he set out to put my mind at ease by answering them.

I listened, both concerned and interested, as he talked at length about how the dog would be trained – if it *was* suitable for police work – and how it would live with him at home as his family pet as well as his workmate.

When he finished what sounded like a well-rehearsed piece I felt I had to tell him the truth: that homing a dog as a working dog wasn't something that had occurred to me. I would have to think about it and discuss it with my wife and then get back to him.

He understood, he said. But if he came to see us he was sure he would be able to put us at our ease. He could pop round in the morning.

'Erm... OK,' I said.

It is hard to say no to a policeman.

The phone was ringing.

Just as I got to it in the hall, someone banged on the front door.

I looked at the phone, then turned my head towards the front door, then back to the phone and then back to the front door: which first?

Our advert on the board had still produced only the one – astonishing – reply. Perhaps someone else had now seen it. The phone won.

'Hello.'

''Allo,' responded my caller. 'I 'ope you can understan' me.'

It was a woman's voice. She sounded elderly.

'Yes, I think I can understand you.'

'I've got to 'ome my 'og.'

'I see.'

''Is name is 'am.'

The name 'Sam' seemed to be in fashion – there was a Sam the Labrador and a Sam the Dalmatian in our village – and I guessed this was what the caller was trying to tell me. It sounded as if conversation was not going to be easy but of course I was sympathetic if someone had a speech impediment that made it difficult to talk.

"E's got to go today. Only youngster – into everythin'. 'E's driving me mud.'

This was not going to be a quick phone call. I asked my caller to excuse me for a moment as there was somebody at the front door.

Opening the door revealed a big, black American MPV parked on the drive. I looked about but couldn't see anybody. But in the rear of the vehicle, behind the third row of seats, four ears could be seen sticking up. I couldn't resist taking a peep. I pressed my nose against the window in the tailgate. Two pairs of eyes stared back at me.

They belonged to two young German Shepherds whose appearance was so striking I was taken aback. Their coats were black and tan, but with hardly any black compared to other Shepherds, and much of the 'tan' was more like cream. Even if I hadn't been told they were brother and sister, their rare colouring meant they had to be related. I wondered if they were American bred.

A tall, slim man appeared from round the corner of the house.

'Oh, hi,' he said, raising a hand in a gesture of greeting. 'I went round to try the back door, I hope you don't mind. I'm looking for Barrie.'

'Oh, hello.' I hoped I sounded welcoming but I was distracted by the thought that it was nine o'clock and I was sure I had arranged with the American chap to bring the dogs at ten o'clock.

'I'm Bob Kerry. I've brought you Wilma and Rob. I'm sorry I'm so early. I just felt I had to get them out – I'd told the police they were gonna go yesterday.'

'I'm on the phone, actually,' I said. 'Would you just give me a moment?'

But Mr Kerry wasn't looking at me; he was staring at a car coming slowly up the village street, a police car. It stopped at the end of our drive.

I hurried back to the phone and snatched it up. 'I'm sorry to have kept you waiting.'

'Oh, hello,' I heard clearly from a voice that spoke without hesitation. I furrowed my brow. It sounded as if my caller had had a miraculous recovery.

'I thought it would be easier if I spoke to you instead of my mother,' said the new voice.

I was beginning to feel I was having a confusing morning.

'My mother needs to rehome her dog. He's only four months old and I'm afraid she can't cope with him. Matters came to a head last night. Mother had taken her teeth out, just for a minute or two, when she suddenly heard the sound of crunching. Mother would like another word.'

'It's me again,' said the original voice. 'Ooh, what has he got now, I thought. And there they were – in bits all over the 'arpet. Cost me three 'undred pounds. "Oh you naughty boy," I said to him.'

His owner went on to recap further exploits, some of which I could follow, and she was clearly at the end of her tether. Dorothy was feeling well enough to drive now and I arranged for her to collect the youngster that afternoon.

Having agreed to take 'am, I could now give my attention to Mr Kerry and I went out to join him. I found him staring open-mouthed. An officer had left the police car and was proceeding down the drive.

He stopped when he got to Mr Kerry's MPV and ran his eye over it. Then he spotted me and called out, 'Mr Hawkins!' I nodded in acknowledgement. He came across to me, hand extended. 'Charlie Morecambe.'

We shook hands and he turned to Mr Kerry, who had a worried expression.

'It's all right, Mr Kerry,' I said. 'PC Morecambe's come to see a dog – he's not been trailing you!'

Mr Kerry rested a hand on my shoulder.

'He had me worried there... I thought, Have the British police got time to follow me around to see if I've given up my dogs?'

I smiled in commiseration. I wasn't the only one having a confusing morning.

Dorothy had been out walking Pearl when our callers had arrived. As a dog handler, on a scale of one to ten I probably rated two at that time whereas Dorothy probably rated 50, so when she came back I left her to deal with the pair of new arrivals while I dealt with PC Morecambe.

Before I introduced our first ever orphan to the policeman I wanted to know rather more than I had been told on the phone about the life of a police dog. I invited him in for a coffee.

As we sat talking, a realisation struck me. For the first time I appreciated the full enormity of what I had undertaken. That in my hands lay the future of this dog. What happened to him for the rest of his life depended on me and my making the right decision. As PC Morecambe spoke in detail and at length about what was involved with the training, I was gazing at the floor, finding it hard to pay attention, struck by the weight of the responsibility I had – so lightly – undertaken. Then suddenly I thought, Pay attention to what he is saying. Now you've realised what you've taken on, you have to weigh up this man. I looked up and concentrated on the man and what he was saying.

'... and for the right dog it's a marvellous life,' I heard.

Then he fell silent. My penetrating look must have thrown him off track.

I ran my eye over him; which was ironic, because that must be what a policeman does to a suspect.

He had a button missing off his shirt, his hair stuck up at the back of his head as if he had only bothered to comb the front, and his serge trousers showed no signs of a crease, but did show what looked like grass stains on the knees.

I had a sudden thought: When we parted with the dogs we rehomed, would we ever see them again? This prompted me to ask him if he lived locally.

Yes, he lived in Fox Fen, near the reservoir, which was handy, he said, for walking his dog in summer: the lad could have a swim to cool down. He went on to explain that he didn't work for the local force, however; he was with a different dog unit.

I asked him about training methods. I asked him what would happen if the dog didn't complete the training course. I asked him about veterinary care. I asked him about a typical working day for the dog. I asked him how much time the dog would expect to spend in the dog van. I still had a lot more questions to ask and was about to put the next one when he pulled out a wallet, opened it and took out a photograph. He held it out to me.

'That's my last boy,' he said. 'Digby.'

I took the photo and looked at a head and shoulders portrait of a classic, handsome, black and tan German Shepherd. His eyes shone, as did his coat, his ears were erect and his black nose glistened.

'That was him when he was only three,' said PC Morecambe. 'And this was us on holiday in the Lake District.'

He held out another photo. This one was of a man and his dog, out in the countryside, the man smiling broadly as his dog splashed about in water.

And a third photo. This was of a younger, slimmer PC Morecambe, smartly turned out in tunic, pressed trousers and cap, stiffly posing for the camera, a German Shepherd sitting to attention by his side.

'That was when he passed out from training school. He looked fantastic.'

What he looked was happy: bright-eyed, alert and eager.

'Lost him with bloody cancer. He was only six.'

PC Morecambe sat back in his chair, his thoughts now elsewhere. We sat together in silence for several moments.

I no longer had the will to question him as I had done. Not a man who carried with him in his wallet photos of the dog he had lost.

Yes, I would want to have lots more information, but I had the feeling that I knew what I really needed to

know: that this was a man into whose hands I could
entrust a homeless dog.

We went off to meet Monty.

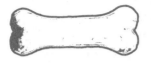

Goodbye

The phone was ringing.

I was expecting a call. Mrs Burton had said she would ring at nine o'clock on Saturday morning, but it wasn't nine o'clock yet. Or was it? I was still half asleep.

I still wasn't used to getting up early on Saturday mornings. Trudging down the hall to answer the phone I reflected on how my Saturdays used to be. I'd read the paper, have a leisurely breakfast, have a yawn and a stretch, perhaps wander round the bric-a-brac market in town, maybe take the dog for a walk, although not too far.

And now... today I had five dogs to walk! My hand on the phone, I paused and pictured the five. And smiled – what a lovely thought.

'Hello.' As I lifted the receiver another thought quickly followed on: At some time today it would be only four dogs.

'Hello, Mr Hawkins. I'm sorry to ring you so much earlier than I said. But I just couldn't wait.'

I smiled again. That was just the sort of thing I wanted to hear. 'Hello, Mrs Burton.'

'I thought the earlier I rang, the earlier we could arrange to come and pick him up.'

The eagerness in her voice was music to my ears.

'I can't wait,' she said.

'You haven't changed your mind, then, about wanting him,' I said, teasing.

'I shan't deign to even answer that question,' was the reply. 'But I have a couple of questions to ask if I may.'

'Fire away.'

There followed a series of questions, all relating to Monty's well-being. For this was going to be Monty's Big Day. Monty was going to his new home with Mr and Mrs Burton.

'He's a cracking dog,' PC Charlie Morecambe had said when he met Monty. 'I'd love to have him.'

He had taken him back to the police kennels for some initial tests which Monty had – of course – passed with flying colours.

'He's full of it,' Charlie had said. 'My sort of dog.'

But the force X-rayed potential canine recruits to assess their hips. Hip dysplasia is a common problem in German Shepherds and without a good 'hip score' the strains put upon a police dog could lead to early retirement. Monty's hips, we were told, were fine for a family pet, but as a working dog there was doubt whether he would be able to scale walls until retirement age.

'I miss him already,' Charlie had said when he brought him back. He'd had him one day.

As he was getting into his police car he had paused, pursed his lips and looked at me. 'If I don't find a dog soon they'll have me back pounding a beat.' He shut his eyes for a moment at the thought. I could tell that his disappointment wasn't just because he hadn't found himself a police dog; it was so much greater because he thought that he had. He was about to close the door of his police car when he looked up at me and said, 'I don't suppose you want any help sometimes, do you? I could do with walking a dog.' He patted his belly. But I knew that wasn't the only reason why he wanted to walk a dog. I had had that same sense of longing when I had been without Elsa after she died. I would gaze at other people's dogs. I would ask if I could stroke their dog. It was a need.

I told Charlie I would be delighted if he came and walked some of our orphans – and I meant it. Most big dogs usually need plenty of exercise and it would also be a chance for me to get tips about dog-handling from a professional.

Charlie's loss was to be Mr and Mrs Burton's gain. And they wanted to come and collect their new dog ASAP, as Mrs Burton's phone call was making clear.

'I can't wait,' she said. 'We can be round in twenty minutes if that's all right with you.'

I had to ask her to be patient a little longer.

'I'd like to take Monty for one more walk,' I said. 'Our last walk together.'

She understood. They would come round late morning.

I put the phone down and stood gazing at it. Those words I had used, 'our last walk together', had stilled me. I realised what it would be: my last walk with a dog that had become in just three weeks my companion, my friend, my playmate, my personal guard. My dog.

Looking back now I realise how lucky we were with our first rehoming, how easy it was. From then on we would be handing over our dogs to people we had met only a couple of times, usually after replying to an advertisement. No matter how much care we took in our assessments, no matter how many enquiries we made, no matter how much more skilful we became in assessing the suitability of the home, we were still taking a risk. We were placing our trust in the people. And people could put on an act. We all do at some time or other. We are on our best behaviour on a first date. We want to impress at the interview for a job. Dorothy and I had something that people coming to us wanted. How much of an act would they put on to get it from us?

Mr and Mrs Burton lived in the next village, where they had seen our advert in the village shop, but before that they had lived in Little Wilberry. Over the years we had often seen them walking their female Shepherd, and stopped to admire her and to chat. From first-hand experience we knew this was a couple who regularly exercised their dog, took her to training classes, immediately whisked her off to the vet at the first sign of a health problem, took her away at weekends caravanning, took her on holiday with them and were stricken with grief when she died suddenly at only eight years of age.

For our last walk together I would take Monty somewhere different.

'How would you like to go to the reservoir?' I said, holding up his lead and dangling it temptingly.

He did his usual rushing round in a circle, then jumped up at me, paws on my shoulders, then another rush round in a circle. He knocked over the kitchen flip-top bin.

I opened the back of the old Volvo estate. He didn't leap in, but waited for the instruction. Standing, ready to spring, eyes fixed on me waiting for the word, trembling with excitement.

'In the back!' And he was up with a surge of power off those back legs, skidding across the carpet in the load-carrying area, crashing into the rear seat. Then he turned back to come and put his head out of the opening, look all around and give me a lick in the ear. I could read the eager, happy anticipation on his face. He stood there, king of the castle. I looked at him and shook my head in wonder and admiration. How I adored this breed.

He loved to learn new things to do, and learnt so quickly. All I'd need to do was go through it with him two or three times and he'd got it.

'You're so clever as well as handsome,' I said to him.

Wag, wag, wag went his tail. 'Are you sure you want to go for a walk?' I asked. I shouldn't have teased him but I couldn't resist it. He held up a paw and plopped it down on my arm which, in readiness, I had held out. Then he leant forward and took hold of some strands of my hair in his teeth. This is why I couldn't resist teasing him. I knew what he was going to do. Just three weeks and we had developed our own fun routines. I jerked my head back and cried out in mock pain.

On the way to the old reservoir I looked in the rear-view mirror. I knew what I would see: two paws resting on the top of the back seat of the car, one either side of the head of a German Shepherd dog. I couldn't see a great deal other than that in the mirror. The dog was looking about, sometimes screwing his head round behind him as we passed something of particular interest. I realised that when I drove the car after that day I would miss that view in my mirror.

I wondered if he would go in the water. I had been to the reservoir with Orphan Number Two, Pearl, the gentle white German Shepherd, the previous Saturday while Dorothy had taken Monty to an old aerodrome. The reservoir is at the top of a rise and Pearl had halted at the top and stood gazing at the reservoir, obviously a new sight for her. Gingerly, she had made her way down to the water's edge.

'Are you going to go in?' I asked in an encouraging tone. One paw had gone forward slowly at the water's edge and touched the water in her usual genteel, lady-like manner. And that was it. The sum of any interest Pearl showed in the reservoir.

Today I reached the water's edge before Monty, the boy having been distracted and led away across two fields by a hare. He never caught anything. It was clear that wasn't the intention; he wasn't in determined pursuit. The chase was just fun.

I stood at the water's edge, alert for the sound of running footsteps behind me; I had no intention of being tipped into the water and soaked.

I liked it there. It was a reservoir created long ago by a farmer to supply water to his fields of 'tatties', as the locals called potatoes. Created by human beings for the purposes of large-scale agricultural production, it had over the years been colonised by wildlife. It was now either a home or a stopping-off point for many birds and small creatures that I could see and no doubt for far more tiny living things that I couldn't. The rise on which the reservoir was sited was very exposed and often when we walked there the wind would cause waves on the water, which brought to mind summer days on the beach. Today the water was still. It was spring and I watched a mother bird glide across the water followed behind by a line of youngsters. I recalled that Dorothy had told me on our first visit to the reservoir that these little brown birds were grebes.

Suddenly, Monty shot past a few yards away, not close enough for me to have heard him approach. Coming face to face with this expanse of water he braked hard at the edge of the bank. He turned round to look at me as if to say, What's this? Then he ran towards me, turned as he got to me and leapt off the bank.

SPLASH!

'Aaaooooooooooooowww!' I cried out.

I could never have foreseen the force with which he hit the water and the volume of water he displaced. I tottered about, horrible muddy water coating my spectacles. I couldn't see a thing. Dirty cold water covered my face and my hair, soggy cold trousers and shirt clung to my skin.

I was going to miss this dog.

We sat in the living room, Mr and Mrs Burton, Dorothy and I, drinking tea.

'I wasn't going to have another one,' Mrs Burton said. 'I couldn't face going through that pain again when you lose them...'

Her voice trailed off and she turned her head away. It had been several months since she had come down one morning to find Sophie had died overnight in her basket. Her husband, Trevor, placed a hand on her arm, then looked at Dorothy and me.

'We buried her at the bottom of our garden. Mary still goes down every day to her grave.'

It was time to lighten the tone of the conversation and look to the future. We changed the subject to Monty.

'He's going to be very different, this one,' Dorothy said to them both. 'But then you know that.'

'Oh, yes!' Mary said, smiling. The sombre atmosphere had been broken by the thought of Monty and his antics.

She reached down and picked up a bulging carrier bag she had brought with her. She pulled out a leather lead in royal blue, then a blue collar, both with price tickets attached.

'And I went into town this morning, early,' she said, 'and had a disc engraved to put on his collar.'

A chill went through me. Were they going to change his name? I suddenly remembered the promise I had made to homeless John, who had had to give up Monty. I hadn't thought to tell Mary and Trevor about this promise on their previous visits to see Monty. There had been so much else to tell them and to ask them. I hoped fervently now they didn't dislike his name and were giving him a new one.

Mary was holding a round metal disc. From where I was sitting it seemed to have a fancy edging.

'That looks nice,' I said. 'Can I see?'

She passed the disc to me. On one side was the name and telephone number of the new owners. I turned the disc over. It was blank. I looked up.

'We haven't put his name on it,' said Mary. 'I read somewhere that you shouldn't put the dog's name on. It makes it easier to steal the dog. They can use his name when handling him.'

I nodded in agreement.

'And nobody's likely to guess his name is Monty,' she said.

Would he get in their car?

The four of us were standing on the drive. Monty sported his new collar and his new lead.

'This is the third time he's met you,' Dorothy said to Mary and Trevor, 'and he was pleased to see you today – I think he'll go with you.'

It was when Dorothy said, 'I think he'll go with you,' that a feeling of misery welled up in me. He was going.

'Can I just have a minute with him alone?' I said to the other three.

Mary nodded knowingly.

'Of course,' said Trevor. 'Do you want us to go back indoors?'

'No, it's all right,' I said. 'I'll just walk him to the end of the drive.' I turned to Monty. 'Come on, mate.'

He trotted with me up to the gate. I knew how eager his new owners were. I couldn't keep them waiting long. We turned away from the gate, walked a few yards and stopped. I asked Monty to sit, so I could squat down and make a fuss of him.

He had been a companion for me in those last days when Dorothy had been in hospital. Out on our walks off-lead he tore about, into this, into that, crashing through hedges, excitedly following a trail, leaping up at the tree after a squirrel. But of an evening we had sat together in the kitchen and I had discovered that this rambunctious dog could sit, still like a statue. I would put my face close to his and speak quietly to him. And I would put my hand on his head and slowly run it down the length of his body. And then again. And then again. When I stopped he would turn his head and fix me with a look. And I would do it some more.

Here we were now, out on the public highway, a trio of people watching us from the garden. But Monty was as still as if we were alone together in the kitchen at night. If you were to ask me now, having been the proud owner of so many German Shepherd dogs, what is the most striking characteristic of the breed, I would reply as follows. I would not say, as is the popular misconception, that they are naturally aggressive. I would not say that their most striking characteristic is the ability to learn quickly, although of course they do – and some of them seem to have more brains than their owners. And yes, they want to please you. Yes, they want to be with you. Yes, to the kind and caring owner they are devoted. But it is the German Shepherd's sensitivity that always astonishes me, including this big, bruising, rushing-about, gambolling teenager, Monty. Now he had picked up my sombre mood.

He offered me his paw and gazed at me. I am not imagining it when I say he looked at me quizzically: he tilted his head, first one way then the other. For three weeks he had been my dog. How long does it take before you come to love your dog? My chest started to heave and I took a couple of gulps.

I knew how long.

Squashing My Foot

'I think a lot of men are not very good with poo.'

It was Dorothy's voice I overheard. I was drying Lion-Maned Dog's feet in the utility room, which was not a straightforward job because as far as he was concerned it was another new game.

'But Peter does my head in.' That was Cecilia, who a few hours earlier had brought the Lion-Maned Dog, our Orphan Number Seven, to us.

'More tea?' asked Dorothy.

They were having a nice cup of tea and a chat in the kitchen while I attempted to towel a dog nearly as big as the utility room we shared.

'Go on, then,' said Cecilia. 'And can I nick another chocolate digestive?'

Save one for me, I thought on hearing that.

'Our garden's too big to mow it every week,' said Cecilia. 'And the grass gets tall and you can't see where the dogs have been. Yorkies only do little poos anyway compared with the dogs you have, but Peter just can't bring himself to pick them up.'

Lion-Maned Dog gave me a wet lick in my left ear as I kneeled down to pick up a back leg.

'Urgh!'

'You all right in there, darling?' called out Dorothy.

'Oh yes, I'm having a great time. He trod on my foot just now – he weighs a ton. I don't think he knew he was standing on it – I had to pull his leg off. And he turned round and squashed me against the wall.'

'I did offer to help but you said there wasn't room for both of us with him.'

'Oh, I'm all right. You enjoy your tea and biscuits.'

'Thanks, we will.'

'He's a bit of a martyr, your Barrie, isn't he?' said Cecilia in a lowered voice, but not so low I couldn't hear.

'I offered not to go to my evening class but he insisted he would be fine,' said Dorothy.

'You couldn't miss the first class,' I protested through the door.

'So how many dogs have you taken up to now, Dorothy?' Cecilia asked.

'That lad is Number Seven,' Dorothy said. She counted them off on her fingers as she said the name of each: 'Monty, Pearl, Claude, brother and sister Wilma and Rob, Sam and this boy with no name but who will have one soon.'

'I've lost count of how many I've done,' said Cecilia. It wasn't a boast. 'Is this class you're going to for dog training?'

'No!' I answered for Dorothy through the door. 'You won't believe it! Trampolining! Not two months after her operation. UUURRGGHHH!' Lion-Maned Dog had shaken himself.

'Are you sure you're OK, darling?' Dorothy enquired.

97

'Whatever is he doing in there?' asked Cecilia.

'He's just shaken himself all over me!'

We'd had to bath him before he could come in the house. But the dirt in his coat was oil, so too were big dark patches on each of his hind legs. Thinking about my own visits to our local car breakers' yard, there were always patches of oil on the ground and it must have been the same at Lion-Maned Dog's former home. So the first job when Dorothy had got back from her evening class had been to get out the dog shampoo and the hose. Thank goodness it was now summer and we could wash him down in the garden – putting him in the bath didn't bear thinking about.

It had been another great game, perhaps even better than the one where I have to land on him out of the sky. He obviously loved the attention. Dorothy had lathered him all over, then rinsed him off, lathered him all over again, rinsed him off again, but as I rubbed him down now with the towel I could see it was going to take more than one bath to get rid of years of oil and grime. Still, the dark patches were grey now rather than black and at least we wouldn't have an oily hand after stroking him.

Another shake!

'Ooohhh!' Further towelling was brought to a halt.

'Let me out, Dorothy!' I rapped on the door.

'Is he dry enough to come in then?' Dorothy asked.

'No! But I can't do any more!'

I turned and fixed Lion-Maned Dog with a look. 'Now, you've got to stay here,' I said in a firm tone of voice. I held my hand out and pointed a finger at him. 'You... *stay!*'

I heard Dorothy unbolt the door.

He's not going to want to stay in here on his own when there are people on the other side of the door who could provide entertainment, I thought. I'll back out, push the door open a little way with my bum and squeeze out through the opening.

But as I squeezed my way out backwards through the door, Lion-Maned Dog jumped up at me and put his paws on my chest, with all his weight behind them. The door flew open. I took two or three steps backwards, toppled over and found myself on the floor, Lion-Maned Dog staring down at me.

He was grinning again.

I sighed with anticipatory pleasure and pulled my cup across the kitchen table towards me. I had earned a cup of tea. What a day! A dog from a car-breaker's yard on the loose with no lead and not even a collar, a Scout convention, a suicidal charity collector, my attempt at a rugby tackle, bathing a guard dog who had known me for an hour and trying to towel him in a room hardly any bigger than a cupboard, a huge bruise on my foot, dirty water shaken all over me... Oh yes, I'd earned a cup of tea.

Thanks to Dorothy's problem-solving skills, Lion-Maned Dog was safely back in the utility room while I had a rest. The challenge had been to get him back into a little boring room when the rest of the world was more fun. Dorothy went round into the back garden and tapped on the outside of the utility room window. That he had to investigate, and while he did, I shut the door behind him. Crafty.

I was about to take a bite now out of a chocolate digestive when Cecilia picked up where she had left off.

'Peter can't bring himself to clear up poo if he spots any in the grass. And he's terrified I'll miss it when I go round clearing up. He used to come indoors and go into this big explanation about where I could find it.'

I put down my biscuit.

'He'd give me all these directions. He'd say, "It's about ten paces from the shed, looking towards the garage."'

She turned to me. 'Dorothy says you're another man squeamish about poo, Barrie.'

I felt this wasn't entirely fair.

'Well,' I said, 'I don't wake up of a morning and think, Oh good, today's the day I'm going to go round the garden picking up poo.'

'Peter was giving me such complicated directions one day,' Cecilia went on, 'I said to him, "Why don't you draw me a map?" And he did!'

I looked across at Dorothy. I liked it when Cecilia talked about her husband, Peter; it made me seem more normal.

'Of course, I hadn't meant it seriously – I was being sarcastic – but sarcasm is wasted on my dear husband.'

'If you're like us,' said Dorothy, 'you spend a lot of your life peering at poo.'

'Well, you have to,' agreed Cecilia enthusiastically, 'if only to see if they've got diarrhoea.'

'Or if you are over-feeding them,' added Dorothy. 'Our vet says if it's a nice solid poo it's probably the right amount of food, but you might be over-feeding if the poo's soft at the end.'

'Oh, that's worth remembering,' said Cecilia.

I leant forward so that I was between the pair of them. 'I'm trying to have a cup of tea and a biscuit here!' I said.

'Just let me tell you about Peter's new system,' said Cecilia, 'then I won't say any more about poo.'

I sighed and gave up. In a battle of wills between me and Cecilia, I always lost.

'He cut up some of his gardening canes and stuck bits of paper on the ends to make little flags.'

I looked at Dorothy again. Her mouth hung open.

'I'm not joking – when he goes out gardening, if he spots a poo he puts one of these little flags by it. Some days the garden's covered in them.'

Reluctant as I was to miss hearing about the idiosyncrasies of Cecilia's husband, I heard the sound of wheels crunching on gravel, and went to investigate. On the driveway sat a police car. PC Charlie Morecambe had by now become quite a regular visitor. This dog handler without a dog seemed to have time on his hands. And as a devotee of German Shepherd dogs – something we had in common – our place was like a magnet for him. The first couple of times he called round it was on the pretext of walking a dog to help us but last visit he had come clean and admitted he was just popping in to see if we'd got anything new.

'I've brought you some doggy food,' he said this time. I saw that cardboard boxes were stacked up to the roof on the car's passenger seats. 'There's more in the boot.'

'Blimey, Charlie, we couldn't afford this stuff.' It was tins of premium brand food. Twenty-four tins to a box and there were boxes and boxes of them. Charlie was already stacking them up on the porch.

'This is great, Charlie,' I said. 'It must have cost you a fortune.'

'Nah.' He took a break from carting the boxes. He unbuttoned the flap on his tunic's top pocket. I knew what was coming next: the Golden Virginia.

'You've already paid for it,' he said.

I shook my head. What was he talking about?

'In your taxes.' He coughed a few times then spread tobacco out on a cigarette paper. 'Our dog unit hadn't used up its budget for the year and if you don't spend it the brass cut it next year, so we used up all the money left on dog food.' He ran his tongue along the cigarette paper and went on to roll the slimmest cigarette I had ever seen. He wouldn't take his doctor's advice and give up cigarettes but had set himself a limit of making half an ounce of tobacco last a month.

He puffed on his roll-up while I unloaded.

'We've got a new skipper,' he said, halfway down the cigarette.

'Oh yeah. Any good?'

'How could he be any good?' He flipped some ash away. 'No one with anything about 'em or any sort of ambition would let themselves get shoved off into a backwater like the dog unit.'

I paused in my work. Our love and admiration for German Shepherds gave this policeman and me a common bond. Perhaps it was this that made him so astonishingly frank about life in the police force.

Whatever the cause, his indiscreet revelations were very enjoyable for a member of the public.

'I think this one is going to be worse than the last. He hasn't even got a doggy at home. Mind you, he does keep exotic fish. I expect that's what the brass thought would qualify him to be in charge of the dog unit.'

I shook my head in wonder.

'It's thanks to him coming you've got this lot,' he said, nodding towards the boxes of dog food stacked up. 'A new skipper might notice all this dog food and wonder how every dog eats sixteen tins a day.'

Now four of us were seated round the kitchen table, drinking tea and munching chocolate digestives. Charlie's visit had been rewarded; there was a new dog for him to meet. 'What a cracker!' had been his opinion of the Lion-Maned Dog. And he repeated it now when Cecilia asked him what he thought.

'He's a cracker!' He turned to me and winked. 'You sure he's not nine months, Barrie? I'll have him like a shot.'

'Don't you think your new skipper would notice the grey on his muzzle?' I said.

Dorothy held out the plate of chocolate digestives. 'Up to what age can you take dogs?' she asked.

Charlie took a biscuit and broke it in two, dropping crumbs down his tunic.

'We're only supposed to take them up to eighteen months but if one of the lads comes across a nice one we often shave something off their mileage. My last boy, Digby, he was three when I took him. Not that you'd have known it.' He paused. 'That boy out there reminds me of him a bit. In fact, more than a bit.'

He looked away from the rest of us to stare at his teacup. His mood had changed suddenly.

'Fancy them not giving him a name,' he said quietly, more to himself. But the rest of us also paused to reflect on that.

Cecilia broke the sombre silence. 'We were talking about poo before you came in, PC Morecambe.'

'Oh yes, as you do. Call me Charlie – I'm not on duty now.'

Dorothy turned to him. 'We were talking about how much of our time we spend looking at their motions, as it tells you quite a lot, doesn't it?'

Charlie nodded and forced a smile. Then he turned to me. 'What are you going to call him?'

I looked across at Dorothy. 'We did talk about it while we were bathing him, didn't we? We came up with quite a lot of names but there was nothing we really liked.'

'It's hard, isn't it?' said Cecilia. 'I've had to do it with strays.' She looked at Charlie. 'My husband's a museum curator and loves history. He always wants to call them after famous people from the past. He wanted to call a Yorkie Churchill.'

'Barrie and I couldn't agree on a name,' said Dorothy. 'Everything I came up with he pulled a face.'

'Well, you didn't like any of mine,' I said in my defence.

'What about Digby?' said Charlie.

This produced a pause.

Dorothy and I looked at each other across the kitchen table.

'Perfect,' she said.

It had been Dorothy's suggestion that we should hold a naming ceremony.

'I don't think we should just start calling him by a new name,' she had said. 'This marks a new beginning for him – the start of his new life. A new name for a new life. We should do something to signify that.'

A naming ceremony? At first I was rather unsure. Then I could see the idea was typical of Dorothy: a thoughtful suggestion, something nice to do, rather different, probably not an idea most people would have thought of.

Cecilia was a maverick character and the more I saw of Charlie the more I began to suspect he was too. In keeping with their characters they both greeted Dorothy's suggestion with enthusiasm.

Thus it was that we four had adjourned to the lounge, a slightly more dignified setting than the kitchen. Lion-Maned Dog had been released from his temporary pen in the utility room, had strode into the lounge as if he owned the place and with his tail immediately knocked the remote control off the arm of the settee onto the floor, batteries spilling out the back.

'Now there's a German Shepherd trait,' said Charlie. 'He's clumsy.'

Other items would be at risk from a clumsy big tail-wagging dog. While I moved these to a place of safety, Dorothy found pen and paper and came up with the wording for our short ceremony. I liked what she had written. 'Who's going to make the pronouncement?' I asked.

Dorothy looked across at me. 'We haven't got the authority to do this sort of thing – I think Charlie should do it,' she said, turning to him.

Surprise registered on Charlie's face. He hesitated before speaking. 'No, it was you three who rescued him. It should be one of you.'

But I studied his face and I thought Charlie was rather pleased at the suggestion. I looked at Dorothy and then at Cecilia. 'Let's have a show of hands,' I said. 'All those in favour.'

Three hands shot up in the air. Charlie smiled. Meanwhile, Lion-Maned Dog had been going through the waste-paper bin and had found some paper that had been screwed up into a ball: he was nosing it around the carpet. Charlie picked the ball of paper up and held it aloft. Lion-Maned Dog fixed his eyes on him.

'Sit!' said Charlie.

It was the first time I had heard him use such a firm, authoritative tone of voice. Lion-Maned Dog sat. Charlie put a hand in a pocket of his tunic and brought out a little white paper bag. Lion-Maned Dog's gaze moved from the paper ball to the paper bag. Charlie dropped the paper ball onto the floor and took out of the bag what I guessed was some tasty morsel, which he held up with his right hand.

He looked down at Lion-Maned Dog and fixed him with a steady gaze. He cleared his throat.

'By authority vested in me as an officer of the law,' he said in a judicial tone of voice, 'I hereby pronounce that henceforth...'

He placed his left hand on the dog's head.

'... you shall be known as...' He paused for a moment. The tone of voice softened.

'... Digby.'

Digby wagged his tail. Charlie's hand was still on his head and now he rubbed that head gently.

'And may you have a long and happy life.'

A Friend

It was a dog that was a hundred years old.

He stood encircled by the vet, the assistant vet, the student vet, the nurse, the trainee nurse and the receptionist.

'How could anybody do that to him?' said the receptionist.

For a few moments everybody gazed at him in compassionate disbelief. Then our vet's professional instincts reasserted themselves. 'Bring him through,' Melissa said.

'Come on then,' I said to him and patted my leg. It was an effort, but one step at a time he made his way into the consulting room.

'What's his name?' the receptionist called after me. I turned, looked at her and shrugged my shoulders.

'Let's get him up on the table,' said Melissa. We had not had from her the usual, friendly, 'Hi, how are you doing?' None of us were in the mood for a cheerful greeting.

Dorothy and I both bent down to pick him up. 'With what he weighs I can manage him on my own,' I said. I put my arms around him. It was like gathering up a framework of bones. 'Come on, lad. Up we go!'

There was no resistance to this stranger scooping him up. Gently, I let him down onto the table. His head hung low. He took no interest in me, Dorothy, Melissa or what was going on. Either he felt too unwell or hadn't got the strength. Or perhaps he was just past caring.

Melissa gently raised his head then pushed back the skin round his eyes so she could check for whatever it is vets check for when they do that. 'What do you know about him?' she asked.

'A young chap brought him to us last night,' said Dorothy. 'He rang and said he'd found a German Shepherd dog.'

Melissa was shaking a thermometer. 'Had he found him, do you think, or was it really his dog?'

That question took me aback momentarily. It hadn't occurred to me that the young man might not be telling the truth, that it might be his own dog. It struck me that the question displayed Melissa's greater experience of dealing with people and their dogs. Yet as Melissa examined the dog I thought it over and felt sure the young man was genuine. He had seemed so shocked.

'He was on the pavement,' he had said. 'I was parking my car and I could see something just lying there. There was nobody about – I was looking around. It was dark but I could see how thin he was and that he was alive.'

I asked him where he'd found the dog.

'Ealing, in West London.'

'London! You've never brought him all the way from London?'

'Yes, I have,' the young man said, nodding. 'That is where I live. I found him outside the house.'

'London's sixty or seventy miles – how on earth did you come to contact us?'

'My landlady knows someone called Cecilia. I rang her and she gave me your telephone number. I had phoned the police and they had told me to contact the traffic warden – no, sorry – the dog warden, but when I rang him I got a telephone answer message that the office was shut. I really like dogs – I couldn't leave him there.'

I was about to ask another question when Dorothy intervened. 'I'm Dorothy,' she said, giving the young man a welcoming smile and holding out her hand.

'I'm Hideaki,' he said, shaking hands, 'but everybody calls me Aki for short.'

'How do you do, Aki? I'm very pleased to meet you,' said Dorothy.

I followed her example, shook his hand, smiled and belatedly introduced myself.

It had been nearly eleven o'clock before we heard a car on the drive. We had almost given up on the young man, thinking he must have changed his mind about bringing the dog. He opened the back of his little hatchback. The dog didn't even lift his head to look at us.

The car's interior light wasn't working. Dorothy said she would get a torch before we tried to move the dog. The light from the little torch showed us enough to shake us.

Dorothy wanted to know how the young man had got the dog into the car. He had lifted him in on his own.

His landlady was afraid of dogs and couldn't help him carry it. Dorothy felt that until we could see more it would be safer to stretcher the dog in. She fetched a blanket and gently inched it under his body.

'Goodness, there's nothing of him,' she said.

The light of the kitchen revealed what had been brought to us: a dog that was skin stretched over a skeleton. He had sores on every leg, his sides and his face. There was pus in the corner of his eyes, a clump of dried pus beneath each eye and stains running away from them like lines of dried tears. The eyes themselves were sunken in his skull. What must have been black fur before was now giving way to grey. What black remained was dull and lifeless.

A dog that was a hundred years old.

What to do?

'Did you give him anything to eat?' Dorothy asked the young man.

'Of course, I hadn't got any dog food so I was going to stop and get him a burger but the place I go to shuts Monday night.'

Miserable as we were, Dorothy and I couldn't help but smile.

'Well, a burger might not have been the best thing to have given him. I'll get him something light. Did you give him any water?'

'Ah, I should have done, shouldn't I!'

Dorothy fetched a small cereal bowl with water and put it down beside the dog. She gently lifted his head so he could see the water if he wanted it. There was a flicker of interest. A few moments more and he found the strength to lift his head and lap a little. A sign of need. A sign of wanting to go on. Some boiled rice with a little gravy would be next on the menu.

I knelt down and ever so gently stroked him. Was it my imagination or were his eyes showing a little more life since the drink of water? I suddenly felt an overwhelming sense of gratitude to the young man well up inside me. I put my hand on his arm and squeezed it tightly.

'On his behalf,' I said, 'may I thank you for what you have done for him.'

'I haven't done anything.'

'You could have left him there.'

'No, I couldn't have just left him.'

'Some people would. Someone has done this to him.'

While Dorothy cooked rice in the microwave I felt the need to be polite to this stranger, to make conversation. His slow and hesitant speech prompted me to ask if he had always lived in England. No, he was Japanese, and a student, studying in London. He had studied at language school here for two years before starting university. Dorothy congratulated him on his English.

'Imagine,' she said to me, 'going to a foreign country to study. Not just in a foreign language – Aki has had to learn a new alphabet as well!' Her interest in languages was showing.

Another small cereal bowl was put down on the floor, close to the dog's nose. His eyes moved. He took some seconds to gather his strength, then he raised his front half up and dropped his head down to the bowl. A few seconds more and the bowl was empty. He lifted his head from the bowl, turned and looked up at Dorothy. He gazed at her for a moment or two. Then he slumped back onto the floor.

Our young friend was staring at the figure on the floor.

'You know, where I live in London it's a very respectable street. You wouldn't expect to find this there.'

I wondered if what he wanted to say, but didn't, was that we were supposed to be a nation with a reputation for caring about animals. For at least one traveller from overseas, our image had been damaged for ever.

Melissa had now taken blood samples and gone off with them somewhere, leaving Dorothy and me with the patient.

The rice last night, and some more this morning with a little tinned food mixed in, had given him the strength, with encouragement, to slowly walk. Being left to gaze at him, to take in the state to which he had been reduced, to think about how somebody had just left him like this was depressing and draining. Dorothy tried to take my mind off sad thoughts and relieve the silence.

'Whenever I see Melissa I always admire her hair,' she said. 'It's really beautiful. I keep meaning to compliment her on it. But I don't suppose you particularly notice her hair – I expect you're concentrating on her legs!'

I always found visits to the vet stressful. I always dreaded a doom-laden diagnosis. But the stress of my visits, it was true, was relieved somewhat by Melissa, six foot tall, blonde and leggy, wearing shorts throughout the year, including the English winter. One day, when I knew her better, I was going to say to her that I would have expected someone accustomed to Australia's climate to have wrapped up well even in an English summer. I wouldn't comment specifically on her wearing of shorts. She was a professional person and I was a client of the practice. Still, I was grateful that she did wear those shorts.

Melissa and the shorts reappeared.

'Right,' she said, in a businesslike tone, 'apart from his skin problems I'm not convinced that his weight loss is due to simple starvation. I'd like to take another blood sample and I'll let you know if I find anything next time I see him. Meanwhile, I'm going to give you something to bathe him in and you'll have to do it every day. And I'm going to give you some cream that you'll have to put on his sores three times a day.'

Dorothy and I exchanged looks. I didn't know what she was thinking, but I was thinking, We've got six other orphans to look after as well – this is getting really time-consuming...

I sat on the floor, on newspaper, in our tiny utility room. The newspaper was because Orphan Number Eight suffered with diarrhoea. He lay beside me, outstretched. I wanted to sit on the floor beside him so I could rest my hand on him. He wasn't sleeping, he just lay there. Outside, it was dark and the summer night had turned chilly. I had put the central heating on so that the boiler in the utility room would keep him warm overnight.

As I sat there with him, all my thoughts of expenditure of time were gone. Never in my life had I felt so sorry for any living thing.

I could see all his ribs, and his hip bones stuck out so much I could grip them. I wanted to stroke him. As my hand slid gently along his back, the ridges in his backbone made bumps for my hand to go up and down. I gave up stroking him.

I struggled to shut out of my mind questions that left me demoralised and dispirited. How could someone have left him like this? And where are they now? Are they relaxing and enjoying a drink down the pub? Or watching the telly perhaps?

I had to preoccupy myself with other thoughts. What shall we name him? The dog wasn't well enough for us to have got to know him, to discover his character so we could think of something that suited him. I would have to find inspiration from elsewhere.

Dorothy put her head round the door. 'That young man, Aki, is on the phone.'

He had rung, of course, for news of the dog he had found on the pavement. I reported back what we had learned so far from our vet. He asked if we had chosen a name yet. I told him I was getting desperate: a few more hours and he would have been with us a whole day and still nameless. Then I had a sudden thought. 'What's *your* dog's name?' I asked him.

'Tomodachi,' was the reply. 'It is the Japanese for friend.'

'Friend?'

I nodded to myself. And that is how it came about that a German Shepherd who lived in England came to be named after a dog who lived thousands of miles away in Japan.

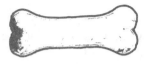

People

'Barrie – blood pressure!'

I continued to stare out of the window, despite Dorothy's reminder.

'Why don't you do something useful while you're waiting? You're winding yourself up. Why don't you make a cup of tea?'

I stalked across the room and threw myself down in an armchair. 'Look at the time!' The clock on the mantle showed ten minutes past three. A Mr Bradley and his partner had arranged to bring their dog to us at two o'clock. 'They can't even be bothered to ring us and say they'll be late!'

'Well, perhaps they're stuck in traffic. Or maybe they've broken down.' Dorothy spoke unhurriedly and quietly.

I sighed. While Dorothy returned to her letter-writing I sat tapping my foot on the floor.

Half a minute later I jumped up. 'It's no good – I can't sit around waiting for these people to turn up. If they don't come soon they'll make us late for the vet.'

'Didn't you say you had an essay to hand in for your night class?' said Dorothy. 'Couldn't you be doing that while you're waiting?'

'They're bound to turn up just as I get started,' I said.

'Or what about young Sam? Is he all right for water?'

At four months, Sam – he of the incident with the false teeth – was being fed three times a day, but his water bowl had to be refilled six to eight times a day. It wasn't that he drank a lot, but after a walk or play in the garden, Sam liked to wash his feet – by putting them in the water bowl and shaking them about.

'Yes, I've given him more water,' I replied. 'And I've mopped the floor,' I added.

'Well then, why don't you go and sit with Friend and keep him company?'

Actually, that was a good idea. 'Yes, I should have been doing that,' I said, 'instead of standing here twiddling my thumbs waiting for these people.'

I joined Friend in his isolation unit, the utility room. We had been alarmed to learn from Melissa that Friend's skin disease was highly contagious; it was essential to keep him away from the other dogs at all times. We had to wash our hands thoroughly with anti-bacterial handwash after coming into contact with him. We must bathe him every day with the medicated cleanser. We must apply the cream to his sores using gloves. None of the other dogs were to come into contact with his bedding or food bowl. All this to do and these precautions to take and the other dogs to look after. And I had a job to hold down. And so did Dorothy.

Stretched out on his blanket, Friend lifted his head up – and there was just the slightest wag of his tail.

'Hello, boy.'

He laid his head back down. I sat down on the floor beside him.

The shoulders with no flesh, the scrawny neck, the patches of dry, cracked skin, the claws that needed clipping, the thin legs, a claw that had been ripped and just left, where now there was a growth that had to be dealt with – I had something I wanted to say to him about all this. I picked up a paw and squeezed it gently. Then I leant over him. I did not formulate the words, they just came to me.

'You're our dog now. And we care about you. What I see is your lovely dark brown eyes. I see your gentle face. And I see this paw. What I see here is a beautiful German Shepherd dog.'

I must have sat with Friend for nearly an hour before Dorothy called through the door, 'They're here.'

A huge four-wheel drive had pulled up outside our front door, but the couple within seemed in no hurry to get out. Dorothy and I could hear raised voices. We hesitated to go out and greet them.

The man got out after some minutes and slammed his door.

'Mr Bradley?' I said, trying hard to put on a friendly tone.

'Yes!' We shook hands. He didn't offer his hand to Dorothy.

'We'd been expecting you at two,' she said.

'Yeah, something came up,' said Mr Bradley.

The woman accompanying him joined us: one glamorous female. Lots of make-up, lots of big jewellery and a heavy leather coat that creaked as she walked. And those high heels were really high. I guessed we wouldn't be taking the dog for a walk across the fields before they left her.

Mr Bradley looked at his watch. It was a very big watch. He was a big man and he had a watch and a car to match.

He gave a forced laugh. 'This is going to sound terrible – we've only just got here – but we'll have to shoot off pretty soon.'

Dorothy opened her mouth to speak – I put my hand on her arm. 'We'll run through what we need to know as quickly as we can,' I said.

He opened the tailgate of his big four-wheel drive. The darkened windows had kept the dog inside a mystery up to now. But there she was: a long-coat Shepherd. Oh, how I'd always wanted a long-coat for myself. She stood up, wagged her tail and came forward.

I turned to Dorothy. 'She's gorgeous!'

Her colouring was more black and gold than the traditional black and tan. I cannot think of any other breed of pedigree dog that has so many variations in colour and appearance. Black and tan, all-black, white, cream, the rare blue Shepherd, the even scarcer palomino Shepherd, the short-coat, the medium-coat, the heavy-coat and the long-coat. Sabrina was a true long-coat. She jumped down and Dorothy clipped a lead on and walked her along the drive. Her coat fluttered in the breeze and she had feathered legs that mud would adhere to later when we walked her in the fields, but for now Mr Bradley had two glamorous females in his life.

And yet it seemed her potential to dazzle admirers had not been fulfilled. Her coat was matted and lacked the sheen I would have expected. She struck me as lethargic, her eyes were dull and she was panting.

'Let's take her in and give her some water,' Dorothy said.

In the kitchen I made notes while Mr Bradley told us what a fantastic pedigree she had, how everybody admired her, that as a pup she had cost him £750, and how that did not include the inoculations, for which the breeder had charged him another £45. No, he hadn't brought her bedding or any of her food with him, he'd forgotten. He was sorry about that, he had meant to after I had asked him.

The woman who accompanied him spoke only two or three times, one of the occasions being to chip in that the dog had American breeding in her ancestors. And that the dog was good around horses: she had five horses. One of the reasons they'd got the dog was to guard the stables – but it turned out she 'would lick any burglar to death'.

While we received all this information Sabrina had found a spot to lie down where the sun that came in through the kitchen window had warmed the floor tiles. Dorothy had taken up residence beside her on the floor. I smiled at them both.

'We've got ourselves a nice, cosy, sunny spot here, haven't we, Sabrina?' she said.

Mr Bradley raised his arm up and looked at his watch.

'Don't let us keep you,' said Dorothy.

Mr Bradley and his female companion went out into the hall and Sabrina got up to follow them.

'What's that?' said Dorothy pointing to the floor where she had lain. A pool of fluid glinted in the sun.

Mr Bradley turned round. He took a deep breath and frowned. 'That's a problem she's got.' He looked at his female companion. 'I asked you to remind me about that.'

'Don't blame me,' was the reply.

Mr Bradley looked at me. 'It's something she's been doing,' he said.

'She's leaking urine?' said Dorothy. Her face had become set. 'How long has that been going on?'

Mr Bradley shook his head. 'Two or three weeks?'

'What does the vet say about it?'

Mr Bradley made no reply. Up to then he had struck me as a very confident man but now for a moment he seemed uncomfortable. He didn't look at either Dorothy or me.

'We have been meaning to take her to the vet,' said the woman. 'We were going to take her last weekend, but we had arranged to go away on the boat.'

Dorothy stared at the couple, a hostile stare. I had not seen her look at someone like that before.

Mr Bradley took a deep breath and drew himself up. 'If you don't want her, just say so and we'll take her away again.'

Dorothy's eyes widened. Before she had the chance to speak I held my hand up.

When we decided to start doing dog rescue work, my wife and I had talked about what each of us was best at and who should do what. My dog-handling skills made it obvious that Dorothy should be the one that did most of the work with the dogs when she fully recovered her health. I pointed out – tactfully, I felt

– that she did tend to speak her mind rather more than I did.

'Well, dear, then you deal with any awkward situations with people and I'll deal with the dogs – that'll suit me fine,' she had said.

Whatever our opinion of these people and of how they had neglected their dog, this German Shepherd shouldn't stay with them. We didn't want the people getting in a huff and walking out with her.

I turned my back on the couple and fixed Dorothy with a look to indicate restraint and remind her of the agreement about our respective roles, then turned back to the couple.

'It's probably only an infection, something not difficult for us to clear up,' I said, trying to sound as casual about it as I could. 'We've got to go to the vet's today anyway with another dog so we'll take her with us then. Please don't worry about it.'

'Well... if you're sure,' said Mr Bradley. 'We don't mind taking her back.'

I wanted to say, No need to put on an act. But I couldn't.

Mr Bradley, his female companion and I went out to the car, leaving Sabrina with Dorothy. I noticed his gleaming black four-wheel drive boasted the latest registration plate. My looking at the car may have prompted him to pause as he was getting in.

'You obviously do good work. I wouldn't like to think you were out of pocket over this – send us the vet's bill and I'll put a cheque in the post by return.'

'Thank you,' I said.

I did send the bill for the three visits to the vet but his cheque got lost in the post.

Death Row

I was beginning to suffer regularly with stomach ache. It was visiting the vet that was the cause of the pain: the size of my bills.

I was grateful that Melissa did what she could to keep the bills down but in reality there was little that could be done other than the occasional suggestion for a cheaper alternative drug or to see two dogs together and put it down as one consultation.

We'd recently decided that as the rehoming work was more time-consuming than we'd expected, one of us – it turned out it had to be me – should go half-time at their job if that could be arranged. So as the money going out went up, money coming in went down.

The number of items on Friend's bill made it look like the week's till receipt from the supermarket. As I wrote the cheque I hoped they wouldn't pay it in that day.

Dorothy read my thoughts. She whispered in my ear, 'Saturday afternoon – too late to pay in.'

Friend's weekend visit to the vet was visit number five. It had been a mixture of good news and not-so-good news. The improvement in his skin problem was there to be seen, the discharge from his eyes had ceased, his tormented scratching reduced now to what Melissa thought was probably habit. But the reading on the scales still flickered around 20 kilos: we had to get to 35. I felt I had to say to Melissa, 'He's had a week now on that special veterinary food that costs us about four times the normal stuff – and he hasn't put on an ounce.'

'Truth is, we've done all the tests we can do here and there is nothing showing up that would cause the weight loss.'

There was silence for several moments in the consulting room. 'So what do we do now?' I asked.

'I'd like to send away some blood samples to a laboratory. I do have a suspicion about what's going on but it doesn't always show up in the tests we can do here.'

She must have read the alarm that registered on my face. She smiled broadly and put her hand on my arm. 'It's all right, Barrie, it isn't something that's fatal.'

'I'm very grateful you told him that,' said Dorothy. 'You know what a panicker he is.'

Melissa's smile broadened. 'I know!' Then the smile disappeared. 'However... it could take a while for the results to come back. What I'd really like to do is to start treating him now for what I suspect the problem is, namely that his system is not properly digesting food. We really do need to get some weight on him.'

From time to time since Dorothy and I had begun taking on dogs, the realisation would hit me of what we had embarked upon and what was involved: the need for animal-handling skills, the element of danger, the demands on our time, the anxiety of letting the dog go. And now something else was really hitting me: the need for money. To add to all this expenditure on one dog, were we now going to pay for drugs and treatment that might not even be needed?

But Melissa had the answer before I even framed the question. 'There are drugs we could prescribe – but they're quite expensive...'

I closed my eyes. Both in resignation and as a sign to Melissa that money was now a real worry.

'... but there is an alternative we could try that would be cheap and, Barrie, can sometimes work even better.'

'Oh,' I said. 'I'm already feeling better myself, now.'

Dorothy had been kneeling beside Friend, gently tickling his tummy. He had necessarily been pulled about during examination, had needles stuck in him and a thermometer inserted. But now, thanks to Dorothy, he was lying on his back with a dreamy look on his face.

'Look at him!' I said, pointing.

'What I want you to do,' said Melissa, 'is to feed him pancreas. It has to be fresh and from a pig. And it has to be fed raw.'

I ceased to point at Friend and Dorothy stopped tickling his tummy.

'I don't suppose you have any reason to know what the pancreas is,' Melissa added. Looking back, I think she must have taken our blank faces to be the result of ignorance of biology, and was being tactful. 'It's not normally used as food. It's a gland near the stomach that supplies the duodenum with digestive fluid and secretes insulin into the blood.' She paused in her explanation but getting no response ploughed on. 'I think in this country you can't usually get it from a butcher – you'll have to get it direct from a slaughterhouse.'

Dorothy and I remained motionless. Melissa looked at us, one to the other. 'I don't know where there's a slaughterhouse,' she said.

'I'm sure we don't,' Dorothy said. 'We're both vegetarians.'

The news from Melissa about our glamorous Sabrina had all been good.

I had, of course, panicked once Mr Bradley and his companion had left.

'Oh, Dorothy, she's been like this for weeks,' I wailed. 'It might be too late.'

'Darling, the dog's a female,' she said in calm, matter-of-fact tone. 'It's probably quite a common female complaint she's got, like cystitis.'

That stilled me for some moments. Then it occurred to me. We couldn't let Friend come into contact with other dogs, so we'd have to take two cars to the vet's and that would mean two lots of petrol...

At the surgery Melissa diagnosed cystitis. 'Clever clogs,' was my response.

'What me, you mean?' said Melissa.

'No, he means me,' said Dorothy. 'I'd been trying to stop him panicking and sending his blood pressure up. I told him it was probably cystitis. And I made him take an extra blood pressure tablet.'

'I've had so many scares since we started this rescue work,' I said, 'I could do with a blood pressure tablet sandwich.'

I was to discover that not all vets were like Melissa. Some seemed to be able to take a more detached view when it came to the welfare of their patients. Even, perhaps, when it came to a matter of life or death.

Mr Treadmore was, it seemed, one such vet, although I never met him. I was, however, to meet one of his young assistants – Luke, who was recently qualified. There was a message from him on the answer machine when we got back home with Friend and Sabrina. He said I didn't know him, he'd got my number from a woman called Cecilia who said I would be discreet, would I please ring him as soon as possible, it was urgent but he didn't want to say any more for now. Puzzled, I rang him immediately.

'I couldn't say too much earlier,' he said when I phoned. 'My boss, Mr Treadmore, was still here. I've got a young dog that's been brought in for euthanasia. He's got a lovely temperament. The nurse on duty with me today knows him and says he's fine with people and dogs – and even with cats.'

'What's wrong with him?' I asked. 'Why has he got to be euthanised?'

'He hasn't got to be euthanised, Mr Hawkins. Jess is a happy, healthy, one-year-old dog. The owner wants him destroyed because his girlfriend has left. His girlfriend loves Jess so the guy wants to destroy him to get back at her.'

I shook my head in wonder at the things people were capable of doing.

'Hello,' said Luke, 'are you still there?'

'Yes – sorry – you'd taken my breath away.'

Luke was the newest recruit to the large successful London practice of which Mr Treadmore was the senior partner. Mr Treadmore had had a disagreement with his young assistant when Luke reported that Jess had been brought in for euthanasia.

'This is the first time this has happened to me,' Luke told me. 'Treadmore claims if we don't euthanise him somebody else will. And there's no point in me refusing – he will do it himself. He said in English law the dog was a piece of property and like any other piece of property the owner could destroy it if he wanted. He said if I wanted to destroy my pen I could. It was up to me, it was my property, and in that respect the dog was no different.'

It was Saturday teatime. Their surgery would be closing shortly. If they were open on Sunday I could go down to London the next day.

'That's no good,' said Luke. 'He can't stay here.'

'You've only got to keep him there one night,' I said.

'He can't stay here in case someone sees him. I told his owner and my boss that I'd done it. They think he's dead.'

'Barrie,' Dorothy said, 'I do sometimes think it's a definite disadvantage you having a law degree.'

'What?'

'You worry over things other people don't give a thought about.'

I gave a contemptuous snort. Still, it was true that in the three days since I had collected Jess, in the dark, from what should have been his place of execution, I had worried over the legalities of it all. The churning over in my mind about the legal implications and consequences had started on the drive back from London.

What was the definition of theft? As a law lecturer my special subject was the Law of Contract. My distaste for criminal law had kept me away from the subject since my student days. Going back in time I seemed to remember, 'A person is guilty of theft if he dishonestly appropriates property belonging to another.'

I never doubted for a second that what I had done was morally right. There was no valid reason to euthanise this young dog. And to do so as an act of vengeance was despicable. I sighed. I knew enough about the law to know that the law and what was morally right did not always coincide.

I went through the legal situation with Dorothy. 'As so often with law,' I said, 'the legal situation is very, very far from clear. The law takes the cold view that a dog is "property" but did this dog "belong to another"? As far as his owner was concerned Jess was dead, so can it be said Jess still belonged to him? Perhaps so, as Jess was still on earth. And that presents another worry: What if the man saw him one day? A cross, with probably some German Shepherd in there somewhere, but with floppy ears and tan all over, and one brown eye and one blue eye – he's rather distinctive. The man would think he was seeing a ghost. No, he would realise his vet had lied to him. So was Luke guilty of fraudulent deception?'

'Barrie!'

'What?'

'I'm trying to get to sleep – it's half past one!'

I sniffed contemptuously. 'It's all right for you,' I said. 'It's not you that's going to prison for handling stolen goods...'

On My Trail

Never for one moment when I embarked upon dog rescue work could I possibly have dreamed that I would spend my Sunday afternoon cutting up the freshly dead insides of a pig.

It sat there on the kitchen table. A great mound of slimy, off-white and pinkish fatty pig innards.

I couldn't take my eyes off it.

Only hours ago each pig's pancreas had been part of a living animal. All eighty of them. It had been Dorothy's misfortune to arrive at the slaughterhouse as the last of the squealing creatures were offloaded and herded inside.

Now she was showering – trying to get the smell of blood off her, she said. That had been the deal: she would collect the pigs' pancreas from the abattoir if I would weigh it and divide it into daily portions. As dedicated vegetarians, we had decided to share the ghastly workload.

For some minutes I stood staring at the repugnant mound before me, but I couldn't put it off any longer: it had to go in the freezer. I picked out what I thought was a whole pancreas and grabbed it tightly in case it tried to get away from me. It felt like a squishy rubber sausage. I must have had only two or three fingers round it; it popped out between index finger and thumb, and plopped onto the floor.

I stared down at the solitary pancreas. This one had some blood spots on it and a streak of dark blood at one end. Putting off having to bend over and gather it up, I foolishly allowed myself to wonder about the pig from which it had come. A friend in a nearby village kept four pigs as a hobby, the old Large Black breed. Each had their own character. Molly was my favourite; she was so gentle for such a big girl, even when trying to steal a tasty morsel from my pocket. Gazing at the pancreas, I wondered if this pig had been a female. How old had she been?

I squatted down, scooped up the pancreas with both hands and dropped it on the scales. Melissa had told us to give Friend just a couple of ounces a day to begin with. The plump specimen before me had a length of stringy fat dangling off one end and weighed nearly three times what was needed for a daily portion. I took a knife from a drawer, grasped the pancreas tightly and began to saw a third of the way along it. To no avail. I went back to the drawer, rummaged through it and found a knife at the bottom with a serrated blade about a foot long, which tapered off to a sharp point – an evil-looking thing I never knew we had. I had just begun sawing when there was a knock at the front door.

Relieved to have an excuse for a break from my horrid task, I pulled open the front door to find myself facing a tall young policeman. I must have stared at him in surprise for some moments. I had not been expecting any caller, let alone a police officer.

'Mr Hawkins?' he asked.

'Er, yes.'

The policeman looked down at a clipboard he was holding. 'Mr Barrie William Hawkins?'

'Yes.'

The officer looked me up and down. I became conscious of the fact that I was wearing a wipe-clean vinyl apron that Dorothy had lent me, in a pretty floral design.

The officer was now eyeing the big serrated knife I still held.

'Erm... I was just cutting up some... pancreas...' I said.

The officer nodded.

'I'm making enquiries about a German Shepherd dog,' he said.

I caught my breath.

German Shepherd. Dorothy had laughed when I said I thought I was guilty of handling a stolen dog. And that I could go to prison. I'd told her repeatedly I couldn't see how it was a defence that Jess was supposed to be dead!

'Do you have a German Shepherd dog here, sir?' was the next question.

'Er... yes.'

The officer nodded again. 'May I come in, sir, rather than talk out here?'

I led him into the kitchen. I noticed that he kept a wary eye on that ugly looking knife and slowly placed it on the kitchen table. The officer stared at the huge pile of raw pancreas. Then he gave me an enquiring look.

'You do some butchering, do you, sir?'

'Er, no – it's medicine.'

The officer's face gave no indication as to what he thought of that reply.

Come on, Hawkins, I thought, you've got a law degree, man. What are you going to do to get yourself out of this mess? Think what it would look like in the local paper: LAW LECTURER PLEADS GUILTY TO DOG THEFT. Would I lose my job?

The officer interrupted my thoughts. 'We've had a report of you having been seen with a German Shepherd dog, sir. You were seen in a car park with the dog?'

In a car park? I went and got Jess in the dark and I haven't dared walk him anywhere people could see us since. I take him down onto the droves where there is nobody about.

'We've had a report, you see, sir, that this dog is in very emaciated condition.'

Emaciated condition? Jess is in good condition – what's he talking about?

'In particular, the dog's hip bones are protruding and his ribs are clearly visible.'

Dorothy says that sometimes I can be a bit slow on the uptake – finally, the penny was now beginning to drop.

'We're not thinking about the same dog,' I said, speaking my thoughts out loud.

The officer looked at me blankly.

He's not talking about Jess, I thought. Someone must have seen me with one of the other dogs. Probably poor old Friend when I was taking him to the vet.

I let out a deep sigh of relief and gave the officer a broad smile.

His eyes narrowed. 'You don't deny having a very thin dog then, sir?'

'Oh no,' I said. 'I've got more than one.'

There was a long pause.

The officer reached into the top pocket of his tunic and withdrew his notebook and pencil.

'I must warn you, sir, that anything you say will be taken down—'

I interrupted him. 'Would you like to see them?' I asked.

'I'm going to,' the officer said.

It had taken a little while before the second penny had dropped and I had realised that the officer thought Friend was my own neglected pet.

I opened the door of Friend's quarters, the utility room, and he had strength enough now to pad out, slowly, into the kitchen. The young policeman was unable to disguise the look of disgust on his face, which had been rapidly followed by a look of frozen anger.

It occurred to me that I needed proof to back up my story of rescuing dogs, including this one. The stack of bills from the vet almost did it, then I picked up the telephone and invited the officer to ring Melissa to confirm my evidence. That convinced him I was an innocent man.

The mound of raw pigs' pancreas still puzzled him; my explanation that it was 'medicine' must have sounded unlikely. I explained that our vet tried to keep costs down for us by suggesting alternatives to conventional drugs, and that in this case she hoped that the pig pancreas in Friend's food might perform the function of his own deficient pancreas – which, in the course of time, it did.

The young policeman and I left behind the mound of pancreas in the kitchen and adjourned to the living room for a cup of coffee. He was fascinated by what we were trying to do. He loved dogs, especially big dogs, and hoped one day to become a dog handler. It was because he really liked dogs that his inspector had given him this enquiry to follow up. Had I got time for him to meet the other dogs we had?

He went on to tell me how he'd recently married and how his new wife was a dog-lover as well. She would be envious of his having been here today. When he lived with his parents he had always wanted a dog but couldn't have one as his aunt, who lived with them, was allergic to hairs. Gone was the suspicious, authoritarian policeman and in his place was a relaxed young man, named Tim.

He was chatting away when I took him into the barn to see our beautiful, gentle, white Pearl. He stopped talking, put his hands on his hips and stood gazing at her. As the seconds passed I became slightly uneasy. Had he become a policeman again? Still he didn't speak. Was Pearl a missing dog? I wondered.

'Barrie!' At last the policeman broke his silence. 'You didn't tell me you had a white one!'

'Er... no.'

'Oh, she's gorgeous.' Tim managed at last to take his eyes off her and looked at me. 'What's she like?'

'Oh... she's lovely outside and inside,' I said.

'Are you going to let her out?'

I slipped the bolt and, instead of bounding up to me in her usual way, she ran up to Tim. He bobbed down and she sat down beside him. The pair just gazed at one another.

Eventually Tim spoke. 'Of course, it's what she's like that matters, *who* she is. But a white German Shepherd...' his voice trailed away.

'Like the white ones, do you?'

He smiled. 'I love all German Shepherds, Barrie – but a white one...' His wistful tone said it all.

As he spoke to me, Pearl suddenly nudged him with her nose, violently, and the big policeman nearly toppled over backwards. So she wasn't always gentle!

'Now that the wife and I have our own place, we could have a dog.'

Ah. I knew where this was leading.

'I know Annette would love to meet her. Can I come back later with Annette when I've finished my shift?'

'Tim, I know you're a policeman but you still have to pass our vetting system.'

He nodded his head enthusiastically. 'I'd expect no less.'

Tim and Annette came and walked Pearl three or four times before they adopted her.

And that was how it came about that our Orphan Number Two had been found a home. Not by our advert on the board in the next village, although I reflected afterwards that was ironic. Tim lived in that village, got his newspapers from the shop, and often scanned the board, but had managed to miss our notice seeking homes for our orphans. And how ironic it also was that Dorothy and I had been suspected of cruelty and neglect. Like so many others who perpetrate these wrongs, the person or persons who so neglected Friend were never apprehended and prosecuted, but those who had helped him became objects of suspicion and were investigated and questioned. Later though, I was to take some comfort from that. I was pleased that someone who had seen me with the dog in that state had taken the trouble to report us to the police and that they had taken the trouble to investigate.

Shortly afterwards, Tim was promoted and they moved away, but we were to see Pearl and Tim and Annette again. When we had been doing the rescue work for nearly a year, a group of friends who ran a dog-training club held a fun dog show, part of the proceeds of which they kindly donated to pay some of our vet and kennel fees. And Tim and Annette brought Pearl along, so we could see how she had blossomed, how happy she was, how she adored Tim and Annette and how they adored her.

It had taken only a few days for her to settle in to her new home and I telephoned Sarah Phipps, who had had to part with her beloved dog before going into hospital. The phone rang without being answered on a number of occasions but one day it was answered by a man. He said he was Sarah's cousin. I told him that she had brought Pearl to us for rehoming. He knew all about it. I was ringing now, I said, to let her know that

Pearl had been rehomed and had settled in well with her new family.

'I'm sorry to have to tell you,' the man said, 'but Sarah died two days ago. I know how grateful she was that you had taken her dog.'

When I saw Pearl at the fun dog show and saw how well she was, and how happy, I wished that Sarah Phipps could have seen her.

Different People

'I could kiss you,' I said.

'Wow! Good job Dorothy's not here then,' said Melissa.

Hmm. I realised I was getting a bit carried away. But I could have jumped in the air. Thanks to Melissa, not one, but two of our orphans were homed!

I'd called in to the surgery to give her a box of chocolate toffees as a token of our gratitude.

Our vet's double strike had begun with a curious phone call.

'Barrie,' she had said. 'I may have found a home for one of your dogs.'

'Really? Oh, Melissa, we need it – we've still got Claude, Wilma and Rob, Sam the Teeth, and Digby – oh, and of course Friend, but obviously he's not ready to be homed.' I was about to add our latest acquisition, Jess, to the list but thought better of it. Melissa wouldn't be very pleased if she was found guilty of conspiracy to handle stolen goods.

'They're a lovely couple, clients of ours,' said Melissa. 'They've recently lost their dog. I can recommend them one hundred per cent. Their names are George and Cliff. They're a gay couple. But...'

Her voice trailed off. So there was a 'but'.

'I'm afraid you might be put off.'

'Because they're gay? No way.'

'No, no, not because of that. It's more... their... their appearance.'

'Their appearance?' I began to speculate in my thoughts as to what George and Cliff might look like.

'Melissa,' I said. 'I don't care if they turn up here naked – all I want to know is that they'll give a caring home to one of our orphans.'

'You need have no concerns on that score.'

Melissa paused.

'Oh, well, I'm sure I'm worrying about nothing,' she said. 'You won't judge a book by its cover...'

'Hello! Hellooo! Anybody home?'

Somebody was calling through the letter box. I put my soup spoon down and looked out of the living room window. I couldn't see who was at the front door but I could see a man standing on the drive. Never mind my soup. This might be a prospective home. Is it the clients Melissa has sent to see us? But I thought she said it was a gay couple – and the voice at the letter box sounded distinctly female. I opened the door just as a woman was about to call through the letter box again. She straightened up.

'Oh good – you are here!'

'Hello,' I said.

'Hello, my dear. I hope I've got the right place. I'm so glad to see you if I have.'

She was a big woman, with ruddy cheeks, dressed all in white: a white coat, white trousers, white Wellington boots. She turned to look behind her.

'That's my husband, Ron,' she said. 'I had to get him to help me.'

Ron nodded and gave me a smile.

'You are the people that take in dogs, aren't you? Don't tell me you're not – please! One of my customers said this was the place.'

The woman turned to her husband. 'Ron, go and have a look and see if she's all right.' The man set off down the drive to a small Rover hatchback parked in the road. Now I looked at it I could see a dog on the back seat with her nose pressed up against the window.

'I couldn't put her in the van with all the fish. I had to rush home and get the car. She was wandering on the road.'

We let the dog out of the car. She had the classic black and tan colouring of the German Shepherd, but with added grey: she had a grey muzzle and, when she walked, the stiffness of an elderly dog.

'I'm Elaine,' said the woman. 'I'm the fish lady. I call once a week to all the villages round here, although I don't stop here because you've got no pub car park for me to pull on to.' She turned and looked at the dog. 'Hasn't she got such a gentle face?'

She certainly had. And big, dark, liquid eyes. But she was underweight. Her coat was dull and she was looking about her nervously. No doubt she wondered where she was and who these people were.

Elaine had spotted her on the A-road that led to the nearby town, a road with a long straight segment that encouraged drivers to speed. She had pulled over in her van and tried to get the dog to come to her, but to no avail. Even if she could have caught hold of the dog, a van full of fresh fish for human consumption and a dog don't go together. By the time Elaine returned with her car the dog had moved from the side of the road to the middle. This time she was armed with some fish off-cuts and the dog had come to her.

I fetched a lead and collar and we led her to a bowl of water that was now kept permanently in the porch.

'I wish I could keep her,' said Elaine, 'but I've got three dogs. I wonder what her name is, bless her.'

'We'll find out, if she's claimed,' I said.

'I think I've seen her, you know,' said Elaine. 'Have you seen her before, Ron?'

Ron shook his head.

'I think I've seen her in Tubley. I think I've seen her more than once on that grass area at The Crescent. I was going to Tubley when I saw her.' She tapped my arm. 'I bet you that's where she comes from. I'll ask about while I'm there this afternoon. Her owners might be really worried about her.'

I took a deep breath and looked down at the dog. 'Perhaps.'

She noticed the doubt on my face and pursed her lips. 'But she's got no collar. Do you think they've turned her out?'

I shrugged my shoulders.

'She's getting on a bit, isn't she,' said Elaine. 'If they have turned her out, you wouldn't want to give her back, would you? And she's got skinny ribs. She might be better off with someone new. You've got a visitor.'

She nodded in the direction of the gate at the end of our drive. A man stood looking about him, presumably trying to spot the house number I kept meaning to put up.

Elaine lent across to me and lowered her voice. 'You don't suppose this is the man looking for his dog, do you?'

The man put a hand to his forehead to shield his eyes from the early autumn sun while he looked up the road.

'I don't like the look of him,' said Elaine.

Ron turned to me. 'You don't owe anybody any money, do you?' he said. 'He looks as if he's come to collect a debt.'

The man pushed open the gate and strode down the drive. All three of us eyed him. He was over six feet tall, wearing shiny leather boots, oily jeans and a leather jacket, with uncombed hair to halfway down his back. He had on earrings, a stud in his nose that glinted in the sun, a T-shirt depicting a wolf, tattoos on his hands, a thick gold-coloured chain around his neck and a loop of chrome chain dangling from his belt. I could hear the chain jangling with the movement of his walking.

As he approached he looked at me and then at Ron. 'Are one of you gentlemen Mr Hawkins?'

I nodded. I thought Ron looked relieved.

The man held up his arm and jerked his thumb in the direction of the village pond. 'My partner's with the bike, just up the village. We've had a job to find you.'

A large gleaming motorbike with sidecar glided into view at the end of the drive. The appearance of the man on the bike was a mirror image of the man before me now, except for the addition of a long, straggly beard and dark glasses.

Melissa's 'don't judge a book by its cover' comment suddenly made sense.

That evening I was standing in the hall looking up a number in the phone directory when the letter-box flap was suddenly lifted up. A pair of eyes looked from left to right and then upwards to rest upon me.

'Oh, you're here,' I heard from the other side of the door. I recognised Elaine's voice.

It transpired that the fish lady had for much of the afternoon forsaken the retailing of wet fish for the role of amateur sleuth.

'This is the lovely old girl's dad,' she said, turning to a young man waiting on the drive. 'This is Mr Hawkins,' she called to him. 'It's him you've got to thank.'

The young man half-raised an arm in acknowledgement, but stayed where he was. He sported a strikingly long ponytail, almost down to his trousers.

Elaine was bursting to tell me how she had asked at the village pub, then at the village shop and then, getting nowhere, had knocked at doors in The Crescent. A retired couple had known where the dog came from.

The nights had already started to turn chilly and Dorothy had lit the coal fire in the living room. Over a cup of tea the young man, Jamie, told us how he'd only had Roxy, as she was called, a few weeks. Someone he knew had given her to him.

'Did they say why they didn't want her?' Dorothy asked.

Jamie shook his head.

Dorothy and I looked at each other, the same thought in our heads. A nine year-old dog might soon be racking up vet bills.

Just after he'd got her, Jamie told us, one of his neighbours in The Crescent offered him a Rottweiler, a two-year-old male. 'Yes, they get on fine,' he said when Dorothy asked him. 'In fact she's the boss,' Jamie added. Dorothy and I looked at each other again. That had the ring of truth to it.

Elaine wanted to stay and chat with Dorothy while I took Jamie down to the barn to collect his dog. Curled up in the run in the barn, she was probably glad of the chance to rest. Her away day had turned into a frightening experience for her.

On spotting her in the run Jamie clapped his hands and called out. He was clearly pleased to see her, I thought. He kneeled down at the wire and Roxy rose slowly, creakily, and sniffed his fingers and wagged her tail. I opened the door to the run and Roxy padded out. Jamie scooped her up in his arms.

'Gosh, I couldn't do that,' I said.

'Oh, she doesn't weigh a lot. And I do weights. I've got the time while I'm not working.'

He dropped her back onto the floor. 'Mr Hawkins,' he said, 'I didn't want to say too much in front of the others – but I feel really guilty about this.'

He knelt down and gave the dog a playful push. 'Come on then – grrrr!' But presumably Roxy didn't want to play because she dropped down onto all fours.

Her young owner looked up at me. 'She got out the side gate. It's my fault – I know she goes off if she gets the chance and I should have made sure it was shut.'

'Runs off, does she?' I said.

Jamie stood up. 'Yes, she likes to go walkabout. She's gone for half a day sometimes.'

'That's very unusual for a German Shepherd,' I said. 'It's a shepherding breed. Their every instinct is to stay with their flock.'

Jamie took out a cigarette case and opened it. 'Do you mind?' he asked.

'No. I'm envious. I used to smoke twenty a day until Dorothy made me give it up.'

'That's why you've put on weight.' He lit his cigarette. 'I'd be really grateful, Mr Hawkins for—'

'Call me Barrie.'

'Barrie, I'd be really grateful for some tips on how to stop this running off she does. Actually, I've never had a dog before and now I've got two and I'd be really glad to learn some tips on dog-handling generally.'

'I'll be pleased to give you what help I can,' I said, 'but better still there's a terrific dog-training class I can recommend. When we go up to the house I'll write down the name and phone number of the club leader.'

'That'd be great if you would.'

'Did you bring her collar and lead with you?'

Jamie screwed up his face and shook his head.

'Never mind. She can have the collar we've put on her and I've a matching lead for it somewhere.'

Jamie put his hand in the pocket of his jeans. 'You must let me pay you for them.'

I placed my hand on his dog and she looked up at me. 'No,' I said. 'She can have them to remember us by.'

The whole afternoon had been taken up with bikers George and Cliff who had fallen in love with brother and sister Wilma and Rob, and with Claude also.

'Two's company, but three's a pack,' was Dorothy's opinion. 'And however would you get three dogs in your sidecar?'

Roomy comfort in the sidecar was of major importance since George and Cliff had taken their previous dog with them everywhere.

'We go hiking a lot of weekends and we always took Lisa with us,' said Cliff, the one with the beard.

At the mention of their former pet's name I turned to look at George. Melissa had told me it was best to steer the conversation away from their old dog as George could get very upset. They had spent £6,000 on Lisa's veterinary care since her diagnosis a few months ago.

'She had a problem with her tummy,' Cliff said, 'and Melissa suggested fresh chicken might help her and I think it did but George and I are vegetarians and cutting it up turned my stomach. The things you do for your dog!'

I nodded in complete understanding.

'We had her cremated when we finally lost her,' said Cliff. 'We've got her in a casket beside the bed.'

George, who Melissa told me was known locally as Big George, got up suddenly and left the room.

It was a few minutes before he felt able to rejoin us. 'Sorry about that,' he said.

'No problem,' I replied.

Perhaps it was Big George having to leave us to wipe his eyes, or perhaps it was that they were vegetarians, or perhaps it was because their dog was still with them beside their bed, or perhaps it was because they arranged their shifts so that she was never left alone. Whatever was the reason, Dorothy and I both felt drawn to these guys. So much so that I felt able to tell George that after my Elsa died I had fallen onto my knees with grief.

They were torn between Claude on the one hand and Wilma and Rob on the other. They came back the following day, Sunday afternoon, to tell us their decision.

'We figure it would be more difficult for you to home a pair,' said Cliff, 'and so if you will trust us with them we would dearly love to give a home to Wilma and Rob.'

'And you've done so brilliantly with Claude,' added George, 'that we know you won't find it difficult to home him now.'

I was sitting on the kitchen floor, propped up against a cupboard, with Claude on his haunches beside me, pressing up against me. I turned to look at him and realised that, as on that day when I had met him in the living room at Ms Jackman's house, I was again face to face with him. But he wasn't barking this time.

Just then he pushed so hard against me I toppled over sideways like a ragdoll and he put his front feet on my chest and licked my ear. I cried out in mock horror and covered the ear.

Yeah, I thought, perhaps I haven't done so badly with this dog since we've had him.

That Sunday night I had a phone call from Tim, the young policeman who had adopted our lovely white

Pearl. A dog had been abandoned on a bypass and as it was a German Shepherd he wanted to know if I would take it. It looked to him to be quite elderly, a gentle female. A young guy with a ponytail had been seen to stop his car, open the passenger door and push the dog out, then drive off.

After I put down the phone I must have stood staring at it for two or three minutes. Then I went into the kitchen to find Claude. I knelt down beside him.

'If I'm going to do this rescue work, I think I'm going to be OK now dealing with you lot... but I don't know if I'll be able to deal with some of my fellow human beings.'

I put my arms round him.

Legal Complications

The Honorary Chairwoman eased herself to her feet.

'Ladies, our speaker this evening is Mr Barney Hawkins, who is going to talk about the work he and his wife do rescuing dogs, large ones.'

Barney? Should I interrupt to correct her? I was seated beside her at the table, so I could touch her arm to get her attention. But could I correct the Chairwoman in front of sixty members of the Ladies' Circle? I had butterflies in my tummy and just wanted to get this over with.

It was yet another wholly unexpected aspect of the work we were doing which I hadn't considered when Dorothy and I decided to set up our tiny sanctuary, and again it was the result of a surprising phone call.

One of the members had heard about the work we were doing, the Events Secretary had said when she rang. Next week's speaker had flu and they needed someone to step into the breach.

As a college tutor I was accustomed to public speaking but my teaching was mostly to small groups and to students I knew well. But we might get a home for one of our orphans from it, Dorothy pointed out. And it could have an educational slant, alerting people to what they should consider before getting a dog, she added enthusiastically. So here I was.

Winter had set in and dark nights with it. It had been misty on those fen roads, and this wasn't a town I was familiar with. When I had arrived there were no lights on in the community hall, the place in darkness – had I got the wrong night? I parked and sat in the solitary silent dark for several minutes. I was glad to see a man in overalls coming across the car park. He tapped on my window. 'You can't park there – that's for loading.' He went off to unlock the hall.

The Honorary Chairwoman concluded an announcement about the arrangements for a forthcoming coach trip to the Hanging Gardens and sat down. Dorothy had suggested that instead of writing out the things I wanted to say I should just write a list of *key words* on some cards. These would be memory joggers and it would make my talk more natural for the audience than my just reading from a prepared script. She had cut up some sheets of coloured card for me. I picked them up. The Chairwoman stood up again.

'There will be the usual tea and biscuits at the end of Mr Barney Hawkins' talk and he has kindly agreed to take questions after that.'

Had I? She sat down and this time stayed down. It must be my turn at last.

I don't remember exactly what I said in that first talk I gave. I remember that Dorothy suggested I put in some humorous bits and that those carefully prepared stories raised a small titter. And I remember that quite a lot of the other matters I recounted provoked completely unexpected guffaws of laughter.

By that stage we were a bit more professional in what we were doing. It wasn't taking us so long to find homes now, for example. Melissa finding a home with clients for brother and sister Rob and Wilma had given us a boost. Dorothy said she realised now we should be advertising in veterinary surgeries, so we sent a poster to every vet in our local Yellow Pages. That had brought us homes for young Sam, our glamorous Sabrina and Jess, who wasn't supposed to be still on this earth.

Sabrina, I was able to tell the audience, had been homed on a farm near the village. Her new owner reported that she liked to play in the muddy farmyard. As a dog with a flowing long coat this necessitated regular and frequent visits to the grooming parlour – where she loved all the admiring attention.

Sam had gone to live at the seaside and every Christmas while we shivered in the winter cold Mr and Mrs Deering would send us a photo of Sam on the beach, always against a background of blue sky and sun.

I took along a photograph of our new accommodation arrangements for the audience to see, although as soon as I held up my 6" x 4" photo to the audience I realised I needed a bigger one. And I lost the thread of what I was saying whenever the passing of the photo among the audience for them to see better distracted me, especially when it was dropped on the floor or somebody had to find their spectacles.

The photo depicted a purpose-built kennel with 30-foot run attached. I knew it would be a surprise to the audience when I told them it was donated to us by an American. It was Bob Kerry's way of saying thank you for taking his Rob and Wilma and getting the police off his tail.

'I think I know where I can get you a kennel and run,' he had said. It was something to do with the housing for the security dogs at his base being replaced every so many years. He said he'd get us the best one and he'd talk his mate into reassembling it for us.

As Bob had bolted it together Dorothy and I had grown more and more amazed. Now we had somewhere roomy, secure and comfortable for a guest. And it was free – and no, he wouldn't take anything for petrol for delivering it or for his time in putting it up.

The Honorary Chairwoman clinked her teaspoon against her cup to get the attention of the audience, who were still enjoying tea and biscuits in their break. 'Can we resume, please, for our usual question and answer session,' she called out.

As the audience came back, I noticed that the man I assumed to be the caretaker reappeared with them, although to begin with he was preoccupied with noisily folding up trestle tables, rather than listening in to the question and answer session.

The Honorary Chairwoman called for the first question and a woman in the front row set the ball rolling. I was pleasantly surprised when soon there must have been five or six hands up.

I suppose I should have expected to be asked questions. Fortunately, those asked by the members of the Ladies' Circle were easy enough for me to answer. At one point Dorothy and I had half a dozen dogs and they had wanted to know how we had coped with walking and feeding so many.

I was able to tell them I had soon learnt a lesson that might be worth bearing in mind if ever they were thinking of having more than one dog: that two dogs are more than twice the work, three dogs are more than three times the work, and so on.

'Take feeding time, for example,' I said. 'If you have two dogs it's not simply a question of putting down two bowls of food. You may have to feed them in separate rooms.' This is in case one is a faster eater than the other and having finished first then wants to go and raid his companion's bowl. I could have added, but didn't, that had happened to me a few times in the early days. The fast eater then developed their waistline – until I introduced the two rooms solution.

Some dogs were what could be fairly termed 'messy eaters'. They liked to take the food out of the bowl and spread it around the floor, seemingly prioritising which parts of the meal they would consume first. When I complained about the mess and the additional cleaning up, Dorothy pointed out that it was only what I often did with my dinner, eating the chips first and leaving my greens to the end.

And then, of course, many of these dogs for rehoming had a history that affected their everyday actions, such as their table manners. Orphan Number One, for example, Monty, who had come to us with his ribs showing, was obviously a dog who loved his food but was also a dog who had an insufficient amount to eat in the past. The consequence of this was that bringing his food bowl out of the cupboard caused an eruption of whining, barking and leaping into the air. The process of getting the food into the food bowl and then mixing it up was fraught with danger. While other dogs frequently managed to knock the bowl out of my hand, sending the contents scattering across the floor, Monty preferred me to wear the contents of the food bowl. I had soon learned to raise my arm above my head and hold the bowl up as high as I could. But this had the effect of exciting Monty even more. One day he sprang off his back feet and head-butted the bottom of the bowl like a footballer heading the ball. The big metal bowl shot up into the air, hit the ceiling with force and dropped down to crash-land on my head, emptying most of the contents across my hair, the remainder coming to rest on my shoulders and neck. It was a bowl of tinned tripe and Dorothy says she can still smell it on me.

I had two questions that night about the complications involved in walking a group of dogs. The first questioner seemed to assume that we walked all the dogs together and I had this vision of me attempting to hold four or five dog leads all at once, each with a large – or very large – dog at the end of the lead.

But even off-lead Dorothy and I could each only take two dogs in case it became necessary during the walk to put the leads on. Experience taught us that with a big dog straining at the end of the lead, we could only hold one lead in each hand. And it was surprising how often we had to call the dogs and put the lead on, to prevent them running up to other people we met on a walk and frightening them, or frightening their little dog, or frightening their little child. And it was astonishing, if you had a big dog with you who did like to rush up to strangers, how many people you could suddenly encounter in an isolated field in the depths of the country: ramblers, people with metal detectors, game-keepers, people out shooting, farmers, farm workers, photographers, birdwatchers, people with buckets out blackberrying, horse riders and picnic parties. I have had walks in the country where by the time I got home I was convinced I would have met fewer people at the January sales.

There were still a couple of arms going up when the Chairwoman announced that the clock was against us and we would have to stop.

'Well I must say,' she said turning to me, 'how nice it is to have had so many questions. There's probably time for just one more.'

The man I thought must be the caretaker was standing at the back. 'I've a question,' he called across the room.

The Honorary Chairwoman looked taken aback for a moment, then nodded.

'If you've got all this time to give to doing things for animals, why don't you spend your time doing things for people instead? They're more important than animals.'

Suddenly it was as if the audience had all been turned into wax figures. Nobody moved. They were all looking at me. And the only sound was the second hand of the clock on the wall moving round.

Out at the front, I stared ahead of me, numb.

For months afterwards that question would come back to trouble my mind. It was to be someone else who eventually answered it.

I didn't disclose to the audience where we had homed Jess.

I'd had a phone call from Luke, the young vet in London to whom Jess had been taken to be euthanised. I'd had by now quite a few nights when I found it difficult to get to sleep, still churning over in my mind the legal implications of what I and the young vet had done. One night I dreamt I had been sent to prison and on my first day was told they didn't cater for vegetarians and the lunch that day was pancreas.

'Barrie, I know how you've been fretting over the legal rights and wrongs of what we did, so I'm the man with good news.'

'Really?' I wondered whatever the good news could be in the circumstances.

'I've got to tell you, Luke,' I said, 'the more I think about it the more convinced I become that we stole that dog from the guy who brought it to you.'

'We didn't, Barrie.'

'Luke,' I said, 'you may be a brilliant young vet but you're not a lawyer.'

'We can't have stolen it from the guy, Barrie – because it didn't belong to him.'

'What?!'

'It wasn't his dog, Barrie. He lied to me. It was his girlfriend's dog.'

My head was beginning to spin.

'Remember, Barrie, he brought the dog to us to put it down to get back at his girlfriend who he'd fallen out with. I've found out now that he told her the dog had run off. It's all come out because the girlfriend came to us with a puppy she'd bought.'

I was beginning to get hold of this. 'Hang on a minute,' I said. 'How do you know *she's* not lying?'

'I'm learning, Barrie, that when you become a vet it's not your animal patients that are a problem – it's the owners.'

I understood that completely.

'I wanted proof – she's got the receipt from when she bought the dog and it's made out in her name. She convinced me, Barrie. I have no doubt Jess is her dog.'

I felt the need to sit down. I never dreamt when I decided to help homeless dogs I would face situations like this.

'Who would have thought it, Barrie! It's really brilliant, isn't it?'

'Yes, I suppose it is.' Yes, I could feel my anxieties beginning to ebb away. We can't be guilty of stealing a dog from someone it doesn't belong to.

'She burst into tears, Barrie, when I told her.'

'You *told* her?!'

'I don't think she believed me at first. She thought after all this time that the dog must be dead, that he'd got run over or something. She's a very genuine person, Barrie. She really loves Jess. She can't wait to get him back.'

Get him back? My eyes widened.

'Are you still there, Barrie?'

'Luke, are you telling me she wants us to give the dog back?'

I gripped the phone. I had just been hit by a thunderbolt.

'Luke – listen to me – I've just homed the dog!'

There were several moments' silence at the other end of the phone.

'Oh... I... I didn't know.'

I had been meaning to ring Luke and tell him the good news that Jess had settled in to his new home with a Detective Chief Superintendent Bulmore and his wife.

I told him now.

'I don't believe you,' said Luke. 'You've homed him with a policeman? You're pulling my leg.'

I wish.

It hadn't been until their second visit to see Jess that the question of Mr Bulmore's job had come up. We need to know about the new owners' work arrangements to be assured the dog won't be left alone for too long but there are so many other things to talk about as well and it hadn't come up on day one. Then I could hardly say to Mr Bulmore he couldn't have the dog because he was a senior police officer and I thought the dog was nicked. And it was a really good home. The couple suited Jess, and he had really taken to them both.

Dorothy had once said to me, 'I've come to realise that when you do welfare work with animals you come face to face with the worst and the best. The worst side of human nature: the dreadful things people do to animals. But we also meet lovely people, those who take them from us and want to put right the wrong that has been done, to cancel it out.'

And Mr and Mrs Bulmore were like that. They didn't know the circumstances in which Jess had come to us but they knew that he needed a home and needed caring for, and they could and would do that.

I closed my eyes at the thought of knocking on their door and telling them it had all been a terrible mistake and they had now to give him up. Because some vengeful young man had created this ghastly situation for us all.

Luke rang again the next morning. Jess's real former owner was going to come and see us. She would come on Monday evening. I did not have a good weekend.

Dorothy and I told her the whole story, except the names and address of where Jess had gone, although I did attempt to draw for her the cottage and its garden to give her some idea of what it was like.

She cried.

She had had Jess from when he was eight weeks old. As he grew she realised she had made a terrible mistake. A walk in the city park wasn't enough for such a big dog. For months she had worried herself over the quality of his life, and whether she should try to find a better home for him. But he was a dog who followed her about everywhere – would that be too upsetting for him?

Of course she was devastated when he had disappeared, but it would be selfish to take him away from his new home where he was happy. A home in the country. And she had learned her lesson and taken a tiny terrier pup from the pound.

Goodness knows what she had seen in the young man who wanted to wreak revenge on her by killing her dog, but he had been a very lucky young man indeed to have had Lisa as his girlfriend.

When she left she thanked us for what we had done for Jess. She gave me a kiss, gave Dorothy a gift set of hand cream, and for our orphans gave us six sacks of dog food too expensive for us to buy. We gave her a photo we had taken while Jess had been with us.

And on the Seventh Day...

The lady had seen our poster at her vet's and rang. By now I was learning to ask a series of fundamental questions, the answers to which could save the time of a wasted meeting with the caller. Finding a home for Roxy, who had been pushed out of her young owner's car, wasn't going to be easy. At nine she was showing signs of stiffness and prospective owners always wonder how long the older dog will be with them. Mrs Duvalier's answers ticked the boxes and, yes, she would consider an older dog.

Her appearance gave me a surprise when I opened the front door.

Dorothy and I talked with Mrs Duvalier over a cup of tea for nearly an hour. Yes, she had had a German Shepherd before; in fact, she had had them all her life and was very familiar with the breed. Yes, she realised it might not be possible to insure Roxy at her age for vet fees, but paying the fees herself would not be a problem.

She and her late husband had lived for many years in South America. Her husband's family had land interests out there. The clothes, the demeanour and the Daimler parked outside on the road all spoke of an elegant lifestyle, such that Mrs Duvalier felt it necessary to mention that she was accustomed to dog hairs on the carpets and rugs.

Yes, she would be delighted to take Roxy to training class; she had always taken her previous Shepherds, it was an evening out for both of them. Yes, she would make sure Roxy's inoculations were kept up to date – she had seen the sad alternative every day in South America. Yes, she would keep an eye on that slight stiffness – probably the best thing was regular and not too strenuous exercise, rather than occasional tiring bouts of activity. Every question was answered fully and to our satisfaction.

Mrs Duvalier commented on how reassuring she found it that we took such care in vetting prospective homes. Then she paused before saying, 'I know what you've been waiting to ask me.' I smiled. 'Go on then, ask it,' she said.

I reflected for a moment or two. Did I need to know? What would that tell me? My eyes and ears told me most of what I really needed to know.

'I wouldn't dream of asking a lady her age, Mrs Duvalier,' I said, 'if that is what you are referring to.'

'You know it is,' she said. And I thought she looked disappointed. Perhaps she had wanted to surprise me. 'What about the other, related question? Or shall I ask it for you?' she said.

We gazed at one another. I realised then the extent of the covering make-up she wore.

'What happens to the dog if the Good Lord decides to take me before Roxy? That was your next question, wasn't it, Mr Hawkins?'

I nodded.

'My son lives with me. He moved back in after his divorce. It was ridiculous in any case my rattling around on my own inside The Hall. He would of course continue to care for Roxy.'

I got to my feet. 'No more questions,' I said.

'Is this where I finally get to meet her?'

'It is indeed.' I went on to explain how by this time a sort of system had been created. There were two main stages to the homing process. The first question was whether this person was someone to whom we felt we could entrust a homeless dog. If the answer to that was yes then the next question was whether this particular dog suited this particular home. Of course, if the prospective home fell at the first fence then it would be a cruel waste of time for both the dog and the prospective owner to meet. A glance at Dorothy told me that Mrs Duvalier had passed the first test.

'I'll call my son in then,' said Mrs Duvalier. 'No doubt you'll want to meet him and he'll want to meet Roxy as well. He's waiting in the car. I'll go and give him a wave.'

At the front door she paused and turned to me. 'It's so good for your health to have a dog, isn't it?'

'It certainly is,' I said.

'It'll make my son exercise more, so it'll be good for him. He's seventy, you know.'

Mrs Duvalier and her son, Julian, arranged to collect Roxy on the following Saturday morning. She jumped without hesitation up onto the cream leather seats of the big, black Daimler, a rather grander form of transport than the small, rusty car she had been pushed out of onto the bypass. I nodded to myself with pleasure. Roxy had gone up in the world.

As Mrs Duvalier was about to get into the car, her rather formal, businesslike manner suddenly dropped away. She leant forward and spoke in my ear, conspiratorially.

'I've been to four or five places, you know – and none of them would give me a dog. They didn't say why, but I knew.' She straightened up and fixed me with a look. 'I'll prove them wrong,' she said. 'And you and Dorothy right.'

Then she took hold of my hand and pressed something into it.

'A Longevity Stone,' she said. 'The local people where we lived in South America said anyone who slept with it under their pillow would enjoy long life. There are two in that little bag, one for each of you.'

'Oh. Thank you.' My surprise must have shown on my face.

'I'm going to put one under Roxy's blanket in her bed. Then she and I will both have one.'

Grey-muzzled Roxy enjoyed another six years of life on her own country estate in deepest Norfolk.

I've still got my stone under my pillow.

We had only one left. Dear, dear Friend.

'Do you think he's putting on weight?' we would ask each other every day. The trips to the vet weren't so frequent now and the scales there usually showed an increase of a kilo or two, except for one week when we had a bad experience, the scales showing a sudden drop until we realised he had only three legs on the platform. He was putting on weight, the sores were clearing and the patches of bare skin were disappearing. He was taking an interest in the world and, most tellingly of all, if you held up his lead, he got up, went to the door and began wagging his tail.

'I think this dog gets younger every day,' said Dorothy.

I'd been thinking the same.

'Do you still think he's about ten, Melissa?' I had asked on our last visit.

'Ten?' She shook her head emphatically. 'Did I say that?' She took hold of his head and had a look at his teeth. 'Give his teeth a clean,' she said, 'and I think he'll be six or seven.'

Just one to home was my thought as I waved goodbye to Mrs Duvalier and Roxy, watching the car disappear from sight – and then a sudden realisation caused me to skip down the drive. I had a whole Saturday afternoon free! No phone calls to make, no trip to the vet, no prospective owners to meet, no pen to clear out – whatever would I do with myself?

'Why don't you take Friend for a walk?' suggested Dorothy.

I stared at her. 'I do that every day!'

'He's much fitter now,' she said. 'You could give him a really good walk – take him somewhere different. It could be the best walk he's ever had.'

My lack of enthusiasm must have registered on my face. So she cranked up my motivation. 'You could go to the old aerodrome – we still haven't explored all of it.' I suspect that my face now lit up at the prospect. Later I reflected on how skilful my wife was at managing me.

'And you could ring Bob Kerry,' she said. 'See if he's free to come with you – he said he would love to go the next time you went.'

So that Saturday afternoon a part-time student of local history, a young American serviceman stationed in England and a recovering German Shepherd named after a Japanese dog went exploring on a World War Two aerodrome.

The day Bob and his pal had erected their kennel and run for us I had left them to go off to my local history class. My casual remark that local history was my hobby had brought building operations to a halt. Bob's grandfather, he told me, who came from Arkansas, had been stationed in Norfolk during World War Two, and had also spent some time at an aerodrome quite close to where we lived – was it possible that it was the one where we walk the dogs?

I had warned Bob that there wasn't much to see now. But when we walked there he shared my sense of wonder and sense of history. This was just one of dozens of airfields that had covered East Anglia in World War Two, most of which had now disappeared, often under housing estates. The land for this aerodrome had been requisitioned by the War Department then returned in peacetime to agricultural purposes. But some of the runway had been preserved to provide a hard surface for farm vehicles and a few of the old buildings were still used by the farmers for storage.

It was a flat landscape and you could walk far enough to put three or four fields between you and any human habitation. Where engines had roared into life to lift giant aircraft into the sky, rabbits now played and scurried about. Every now and then a rabbit would pop out from the crop and Friend would set off in half-hearted pursuit.

'He's not really hungry any more, is he?' said Bob. 'He doesn't look too bothered about catching it.'

But then all the times I've walked at that aerodrome with our orphans, not one of them has ever caught a bunny – thank goodness.

We had a rest on some bales of straw we came across in an old corrugated shed, whose timber frame leaned eastward, telling us the direction from which the wind usually came on that old aerodrome. As we sat there looking across at the lonely landscape, no human being in sight or sound, I couldn't help but picture what had been there before. I had read some of the books about the forgotten airfields of World War Two, written by enthusiasts, and had seen some of the surviving photos in the county archives. Now as I looked across at the fields of winter wheat, for a moment I could hear again the drone of the engines as the planes returned from their mission, as they were counted back in.

It was the first of several walks that Bob and I and one of our orphans had at the old aerodrome. And it was the first of our exploratory trips to other of the historic airfields of East Anglia. One or two had been carefully preserved with watchtower and relics; finding others was a trek through farmland to a few crumbling remnants of concrete.

Bob must have taken scores of photographs and he took them home with him. He wrote to me that the photos and talking of his stay in England had an unexpected result. For the first time his grandfather talked about his time in the services, the missions he had flown and the pals he had lost.

'Our visits to the old aerodrome had a big impact on me, Barrie,' Bob wrote. 'I could reach out and touch the past. There is a danger that we think everything begins when we are born. But we are just part of a continuing story.'

After his return home Bob and his wife had two children. He sent me a photo of two smiling toddlers. 'I hope one day they will come and visit England,' he wrote in his letter sending the pictures, 'and that they will also hear the sound of those returning aircraft.'

I stretched out my legs until I could feel the heat from the fire on my toes. My strenuous walk at the aerodrome with Bob and Friend had left me feeling lazy and content with the world. I had a whole free Sunday to look forward to. Our open fire always soothed me: the warmth, the glowing and the sounds of the crackling of the logs from the little wood at the end of our garden. I curled up my toes and closed my eyes.

It was then, of course, that the phone rang.

I took a deep breath but I had to answer it in case it was a dog in need of help. The phone had become my master.

I could hear the despair in the woman's voice.

'My neighbour has a dog. I've lived here for eight years and I've never seen him take it out. I don't mean take it out for a walk – I mean take it out of the pen it lives in. It's got a kennel and they feed it, but that's all they do with it.'

'You mean it's not been let out of the pen for eight years?' I said.

Dorothy had come out into the hall. She paused as she overheard the shocked tone in my voice. I looked at her and shook my head in disbelief.

She switched the phone on to loudspeaker.

'Hello, are you there?' the woman asked.

'Yes.'

'My friend says it's a German Shepherd, although it doesn't look like one to me. It's a lovely looking dog. It's got a really long coat, I've never seen anything like it, some of its real ginger and the rest of it's like dark chocolate.' She paused for breath.

Where was all this leading?

'Every morning when I get up I go to draw back the curtains in my bedroom and I see this pen with this dog in it. I look away now as I pull back the curtains, but that doesn't help really – I know the dog is there. I start every day worrying about that dog. Please, can you help me?'

'But what can I—'

'The dog warden can't do anything about it because he says it's got food and shelter. I understand that, but it's got no *life!*'

'Have—'

'I told the man one day I would report him to the RSPCA. My husband told me not to get involved. It didn't matter because the man just ignored me.'

'Have you—'

'Someone says his daughter gets on to him about it.'

There was finally a pause. I think my caller had run out of breath for a moment.

'Have you considered talking to him about the possibility of rehoming the dog?'

'Oh yes. I went out to him this afternoon when he was getting in his car. He says I can have the dog. If I bring it to you, will you take it?'

I pursed my lips. At last we were there. It looked as if we wouldn't be down to just one orphan for very long.

'We can take him on Monday, if that suits you,' I said.

'Can't I bring him tomorrow, Sunday?'

Having made arrangements with Mrs Cadbury I put the phone down. As I did so, it rang again, making me jump.

Not another dog?

I grabbed it up. 'Hello!'

'Could I speak to Dorothy, please?'

'Who's calling?'

'Irma. I'm a friend of Dorothy's from work.'

I gave such a big sigh of relief the caller must have heard it. 'Dorothy!' I called her back. 'It's for you!'

I chucked down the phone and went back to my fire. Soon I was in that happy state where the head begins to nod.

Dorothy came back into the living room. My eyes were closed but I sensed she had sat down opposite me. I opened one eye.

'That was Irma. She works in accounts.'

Fascinating, I thought.

'She's got a tiny terrier...'

Where's this leading? Don't tell me they want us to take a tiny terrier? I opened the other eye.

'She and her husband were taking it for a walk this afternoon and they heard a whining. They were in a field somewhere and they couldn't make out where this noise was coming from.'

She suddenly stood up, went across the room, picked up a box of tissues. 'It was a dog. At the bottom of a deep ditch that luckily was nearly dry. She says it was just standing there. She thinks it's a young Lurcher of some sort, but it's very thin, even for a Lurcher.' Dorothy had her back to me while she was talking.

'Have they any idea how it got there?'

'Complete mystery. It was just standing in the water, apparently, nearly up to its chest. The only thing they can think of is that there had been illegal hare coursers round there in the morning and her husband says that sometimes if the dog's no good they just leave it behind. That it might have been chucked in the ditch.'

'But why wouldn't it just get out of the ditch?'

'I don't know. It may have been too frightened.' Dorothy turned round. She looked so miserable. 'Her husband got down into the ditch and it just let him pick it up.'

'We'll take it,' I said. 'At least it won't be with illegal hare coursers any more. And it's a young dog so it's got its life ahead of it yet.'

'Yes. But this one that Mrs Cadbury is bringing us... Year after year in a pen. That's what we do to people to punish them – lock them up in solitary confinement. And even if we can rehome him, he hasn't got his life ahead of him.'

Her face was a picture of misery. We looked at one another but I couldn't think of anything encouraging to say. So I said what I usually did when we were both demoralised.

'Shall I make us a cup of tea?'

The phone was ringing again.

'I thought people went out on a Saturday night,' I said to Dorothy.

'Obviously not all of them,' she said. 'Some of them stay in and ring us.'

I sighed deeply and picked up the phone. 'Hello.'

'Oh Barrie – it's Cecilia!'

She always said it in such a dramatic tone of voice – as if she were making some earth-shattering announcement such as 'Oh Barrie – I've won the lottery!'

I narrowed my eyes. A telephone call from Cecilia could mean only one thing.

'Oh Barrie – you'll never believe what's happened. Some people were out for a walk this afternoon with their dog and they found a dog.'

Wait a minute – this sounds familiar.

'They don't know how long he was there. He's thin and he looks so miserable. Oh, and he's gorgeous. They found him in a field. He'd been tied up to a hedge.'

Tied to a hedge? Not the same people and the same dog, then.

'What breed is it Cecilia?'

'Well... he's brown, and he's quite a big dog so there might be a tiny bit of German Shepherd in him.'

Her voice had slowed from its high-speed, excited pace. She was thinking. She was thinking what possible characteristics of this dog she could describe that might make me think that one of his ancestors

175

at some point in the distant past had been a German Shepherd.

'It's all right, Cecilia,' I said. 'We'll take him.'

'Oh would you, Barrie! I didn't like to ask you. But you know I only help littlies usually.'

'It's no problem, Cecilia,' I said. After all, what else would I do with my Sunday if I didn't take in three dogs?'

Unexpected

In the years to come I was to experience many first meetings with dogs which aroused strong emotions. Sometimes the first sight of the dog would disgust me. How could human beings could do this to them? Often, a few minutes with the animal and I would be shaking my head with sorrow. Sometimes it was anger. Sometimes frustration. Sometimes sadness for both the dog and the caring owner who by force of circumstances could no longer keep it.

In this case it was astonishment.

It wasn't just that someone could confine a dog for years, not just because they could condemn a dog to a life of isolation – what I could not understand, what amazed me and was beyond my understanding, was how Oscar had coped.

It had been several minutes since Mrs Cadbury had let him out of her car. We couldn't risk three dogs arriving together and had spaced them out over the day. Mrs Cadbury had said she was an early riser and would be with us as soon as she could get the dog away from 'that horrible man' who 'usually spends Sunday morning polishing his car when he should be walking the dog'.

Dorothy and I had listened while she had told us what she had seen over the years and what she had learnt from her neighbour that morning. I had been worried at first that, unaccustomed to freedom, Oscar would try to run off – but he stood beside the car as if reluctant to leave it. For several moments he just gazed at the ground. Then slowly he moved his eyes around to take in the scene. Then he lowered his head and gently shook it. Still he did not move away from the car. I went across to the lawn, bent down and called to him. He moved his head slowly to look at me but that was all. Every few moments he would blink.

It was as if he had just woken up.

I went back to Dorothy. 'Perhaps he just doesn't know what to do after all these years,' I said. 'He might have lost his confidence. Another dog might help – show him what to do. Shall I go and get Friend?'

Dorothy had been gazing at the dog, deep in thought. She turned to me. 'You can try it,' she said, but her tone of voice did not sound as if she was convinced.

I fetched Friend and he trotted happily over to Oscar. With his long legs Oscar towered over Friend and it struck me how spindly Friend still looked in spite of his weight gain.

'I've realised what a striking dog he is,' said Mrs Cadbury. 'He is a German Shepherd, is he? They don't look like that normally, do they?'

'I think he may be a cross,' said Dorothy. 'He's fine-boned for a Shepherd and very tall, but he's got a Shepherd's ears.'

'That bloomin' man says he's a pedigree,' said Mrs Cadbury. 'He bought him from a breeder for his son's birthday but he soon lost interest in the dog – kids do, don't they. They used to have a rabbit as well – they never looked after that.'

'And you say he's been shut in the pen eight years,' said Dorothy.

'No – I've seen him in there ever since I've lived there and *that's* eight years. The man said he lived in the house until he was six months and then they put him in the pen.'

'Oh, for goodness sake,' said Dorothy. 'However long has the dog been in the pen?'

'The man's son worked it out from his birthday, he's been in there eleven years and two months.'

I felt the need to stroke a dog and knelt down to run my hand slowly along Friend's side.

'He's thin, isn't he?' said Mrs Cadbury looking at Friend.

'You should have seen him when he first came in,' said Dorothy.

Looking at me, Mrs Cadbury said, 'He's taken to you, hasn't he?'

I gave him a hug, perhaps a bit too hard for a dog without much flesh on him. 'And I've taken to him,' I said.

Dorothy took her eyes off Oscar to watch Friend and me for a few moments.

'I think he's getting too attached to you, Barrie,' she said. 'He's on the mend now. Don't you think it's time we found him a home?'

'For his sake, yes. For my sake, no.'

All of a sudden Oscar came to life – just for a few moments. That day and over the following two or three days he was like a toy whose battery was nearly exhausted. There would be no movement, and then all of a sudden he would move a short distance, then stop again.

Oscar padded across the lawn, slowly, to Friend, stopped in front of him, and gazed at him. Then he sniffed at Friend. Oscar being a much bigger dog, I thought Friend looked a little anxious, but my presence may have reassured him for he soon gave a slight wag of his tail. The stress of being extracted from the only surroundings he had known for years had probably tired Oscar, and he sat down on his haunches, facing Friend.

Dorothy came across to join us. 'He must be bewildered,' she said to me. 'He may find the presence of another dog reassuring. I think it was a good idea of yours to get Friend out.'

I was not accustomed to having my dog-handling skills praised.

Dorothy smiled. 'Don't look so surprised – we all learn from experience.'

I hadn't enough experience to feel confident about where would be the best place to house Oscar while he was with us. Indoors with all the sounds and activities of the household might be too sudden and dramatic a change from the outdoor environment he was accustomed to. But I pulled a face at the thought of putting him in another pen.

'It won't be the same as before though,' Dorothy pointed out. 'We'll be getting him out regularly. Different people and going for walks might be enough of a change for him to handle now. We can bring him in the house in a few days' time.'

For the first two or three days whenever we went down to see him we always found Oscar standing in the middle of the pen, still, like a statue. Observing him from a distance that was all he seemed to do. He wouldn't be chewing a bone like other dogs, or barking at a bird that landed nearby.

When I clipped a lead on him he would slowly pad along beside me, but only for two or three hundred yards. Then he would sit down on his haunches. He was telling me he didn't want to go any further. He hadn't the confidence to go too far from the security of his pen. Back to his pen we would go, and he would resume his position, a solitary figure in the middle of the pen.

I found it distressing to watch.

'I think,' said Dorothy, 'he's shut himself down. I think he has turned off his emotions and his reactions. Such an intelligent dog with nothing to stimulate him for year after year – I think it was his way of coping. His way of stopping himself going mad.'

Was she right? I didn't know then and I don't know today. But whatever were we going to do about it?

After several days' reflection and discussion, Dorothy had a suggestion.

'Let's remind him how other dogs live their lives,' she said. 'Let's start by taking Friend with him on the walks. Let Friend remind him that there are exciting trails to be followed, sights to be seen, ditches to be jumped, squirrels that run up trees he can't climb.'

What happened in the next few weeks was like a prolonged awakening from a long sleep. On the first couple of walks Oscar just watched Friend, then that German Shepherd inquisitiveness took over: he had to go and have a look and see what Friend was up to, or what he'd found. Then, a little at a time, Oscar started to join in.

The nights were drawing in now. Our late afternoon walks were the last before it got dark. It was that time of year when we started to notice the pheasants. All the dogs would follow their scent in the fields. Sometimes the trail would lead to the pheasant, then there would be a flapping of wings and a hurried, noisy take-off would ensue. It was when Oscar nearly caught up with Friend for the first time in one such hopeless pursuit that I realised how far we had come. Here was a dog who was bouncing along, tongue lolling, bright eyes wide. A dog who was now living in the house, and would be waiting at the front door at the sight of a lead, barking to go out for a walk. A dog who would try to chase footballs, splash through puddles and retrieve – in his own time – a rubber ring. It was one day when he skipped through a puddle that Dorothy said to me, 'You know what this means, don't you?'

'Yes,' I said. 'He's getting me wet.'

'It means we can rehome him, Barrie. He's ready now.'

Oscar had been with us for several weeks when we homed him with Lewis, who lived in the next village. It was the first home we had got from that card I put in the village shop months before. I didn't even know it was still there. The lady in the shop said that as it was for a good cause they had left it in place.

UNEXPECTED

He was happy to take an older dog, Lewis explained, as he would be retiring from his post as a clerk in the finance department of the local council and an older dog would be more suitable for him. I didn't say this to him, but I'm not very tall and Lewis was considerably shorter than me, fine-boned and with a gentle manner and, age apart, I felt he needed a dog that was not too bouncy.

The village of Great Fosfen has a long main street which stretches for some three-quarters of a mile, for much of which it has a wide grass verge. One day, a few months after we'd homed Oscar, I was driving through the village when in the distance I could see on the verge a man, running. He was being towed along at the end of a lead behind a big dog that was pulling like a sledge-dog. As I drew nearer I recognised at first the little man, and then the big dog.

I waved as I drove past them and Lewis managed to briefly raise an arm in the air in acknowledgement.

I slowed down. I looked in my rear-view mirror to be sure of what I had seen. Yes, it was a man with a look of exhilaration on his face, a man enjoying the exercise, a man having fun.

I told Dorothy what I'd seen when I got home.

'It's amazing,' I said. 'That dog is twelve years old!'

'True,' Dorothy said. 'But Oscar doesn't know that as he's been asleep all those years. Now he's woken up he thinks he's still a youngster.'

Sixth Sense

It was a puzzle. We hadn't seen Charlie for a few weeks. Charlie, to whom our place had become like a brewery to an alcoholic. A man who could not resist dropping in on his way home to see and stroke our newest acquisition.

We knew there had been a disappointment for him. As his search for a suitable dog had taken so long his 'skipper' had decided Charlie's standards were too high, taken the matter in hand, and required him to take a dog Charlie didn't think would make the grade. During week three of the training course Charlie had been proved right.

'We couldn't get him to bite,' said Charlie. 'Well I suppose they could have done if they'd pushed him hard enough, but I wasn't having any of that. He'll make someone a lovely family pet.' He'd mumbled something about 'doing some admin' in the Unit while filling in time.

I was pleased when I heard a vehicle on the drive and looked out of the window to see the familiar white van with POLICE DOG UNIT in blue on the side. I had been half-expecting Cecilia, who was bringing us that afternoon the dog found tied to the hedge, although I would have been surprised if it had been Cecilia as that would have made her only an hour and a half late.

My plan to spread out the arrival of the three dogs over the day hadn't quite worked. Dorothy's work colleague, Irma, was coming late morning with the dog found in the ditch, but had arrived an hour early as she had forgotten her mother was coming for Sunday lunch. She and Mrs Cadbury, who had brought Oscar, had swapped stories and then had a nice chat, while the clock ticked.

As it was a while since Charlie's last visit, he had some catching up to do. I was able to report that Claude had been homed with a vicar and had already settled in well. It had taken quite a while to find a suitable home for Claude, somewhere where his liking of barking ferociously at strangers could be put to good use. The vicar's church and its graveyard had been suffering from the attentions of bored teenage lads, some of whom had taken to relieving themselves behind the gravestones. Claude was to be first and foremost a family pet but the Reverend Winstanley was also to institute patrols in the grounds, whereby the sight of Claude's snapping jaws might encourage the teenage lads to zip up their flies.

'And Digby...?' Charlie said. 'Don't tell me you've still got Digby?'

Digby. How that name brought back memories. Our Lion-Maned Dog. He of the oil-stained coat. Ex-guard dog. Ex-car breakers' yard. My first and last rugby tackle.

'He's gone,' I said.

'Gone? You mean run away?'

'The only running Digby ever did was after next-door's cat,' I said. 'Cecilia should be here soon – it was her who brought him to us – I'll tell you all about it then.' In fact, there was to be an unexpected interruption before I had the chance to do so.

Charlie's face lit up. 'You got a doggy coming in today then?'

'A dog? It'll be the third today!'

I took Charlie down to see that Sunday's two earlier arrivals. We only made a brief visit to Oscar in the pen in the old barn. His journey and move to us were enough unsettling experiences for one day. Surprise registered on Charlie's face when he saw our next new arrival. 'You've not had one of these before,' he said.

Looking up at him from behind the wire was a pair of eyes that seemed too big for the head in which they were set. And the rest of the dog made such a contrast to the appearance of the breed closest to my heart, my beloved German Shepherds. But Lurchers ran a close second in my affections. Lottie was mid-grey all over, with soft ears, a fine-boned physique and a gentle temperament.

I let her out of the pen and Charlie produced from his pocket a ball he had conveniently brought with him. He held it up.

'Fetch?' he suggested, but Lottie showed no interest. He rolled the ball along the ground and then widened his eyes and tilted his head in the direction of the ball, in what I guessed was supposed to be an encouraging look. Lottie stared for a few moments first at Charlie and then at me. A rubber, pyramid-shaped toy that bounced at random angles produced only a blank expression.

'I don't think she's ever been played with,' was Charlie's conclusion.

And it was a conclusion that was borne out in the next few days. Toys and training aids were an unfamiliar sight to her. But even Lottie knew what a bone was, though she didn't chew bones. She threw them. She would hold the bone in her jaws, put her head back, then launch the bone high into the air to land noisily on the ground several feet away. This Lottie would repeat time after time for hours, retrieving the bone each time. Dorothy, as usual, reflected on the dog's behaviour and produced a likely answer.

'Charlie's right that she's never been played with. So she's learned to play on her own. And with no ball or other toy she's had to improvise. Throw the bone for her and I think she may run after it and bring it back to you.'

And she did.

Charlie gave up on what was, for now, unrewarded effort. 'And what's Cecilia bringing you?' he asked as I encouraged Lottie back into her pen with a hide chew.

I rolled my eyes. 'Goodness knows,' I said...

Dorothy, Charlie, Cecilia and I sat round the fire in the living room, drinking tea and munching chocolate digestive biscuits.

Sitting in front of me, looking up, watching every movement of chocolate digestive, nose projecting upwards, nostrils quivering, was a brown dog. And he really was brown. Brown coat all over, nostrils a darker shade of brown, brown eyes and a brown collar. This was Larry, new arrival number three.

'Oh,' said Cecilia, 'he's such an appealing dog. Don't you think, Dorothy?'

'He's gorgeous,' said Dorothy.

I knew what Cecilia meant. He was the sort of dog that seeing him made you immediately want to stroke him.

Dorothy felt we should discover as much as possible about the dogs while they were with us, so reducing the risk of unexpected surprises for the new owner. Thus we tried to make sure each dog encountered everything on a list Dorothy devised: other dogs, cats, horses, children, tractors, lorries, bicycles and vacuum cleaners. And we would try to give each dog a walk in town when it was busy, such as on market day, to see if he was intimidated by crowds. But taking Larry for a walk in town was extraordinarily time-consuming.

'Can I stroke him?' we would hear every few yards, or so it seemed. The top of his head was shiny where it was stroked so much.

I turned now to fix my gaze upon Cecilia. 'Charlie,' I said, speaking slowly and with deliberation, 'Charlie, would you tell me, drawing upon your professional expertise, what physical features of this dog you think indicate that there may be some German Shepherd in there?'

Charlie opened his mouth to speak. I didn't give him the chance.

'Not the drooping ears,' I said, 'Not the single, uniform colour, not the rounded shape of the body, or the Labrador size? What about that smooth, very short brown coat? No, I don't think so.'

Cecilia pulled a face.

'Well,' said Charlie, 'every German Shepherd I've ever known likes cheese – we could try him with that...'

BARK! BARK! BARK! There was a sudden eruption outside in Charlie's van. I turned my head and through the window could see the van rocking from side to side. I nearly dropped my cup in surprise.

I spun round to Charlie. 'Have you got a dog in that van?'

'Sounds like it,' said Charlie, trying to be as casual about it as he could.

'What dog?'

'My dog.'

There was going to be no more chatting or cups of tea or chocolate digestives until we'd met Charlie's new dog!

I'd led the way out to the van – with Charlie in hot pursuit. 'Don't let him out!' Charlie had called after me.

I circled the van, trying to see inside. An instruction called through the window by Charlie had brought the barking to a halt and the rocking of the van with it. Dorothy had had the sense to stop on her way out to pick up a bag of treats. Cecilia didn't quite share our enthusiasm and was hanging back, near the front door.

'How long have you had him? Where'd you get him? Have you started the training?' I wanted to know! Starting the rescue work had brought the unexpected benefit of finding a new mate, Charlie, and it was a double bonus that it was my chance to get to know up close a real, live police dog. A trained dog, enjoying the variety of a working life, using his intelligence, and all in the service of the community: pursuing and bringing down villains, breaking up crowds of yobs, on patrol while we slept safely in our beds.

'Are you going to show us some of the things a police dog can do, Charlie?' I said. 'Have you trained him yet to bark on command?' I looked across at Cecilia. 'Or Cecilia could play the villain and he could run after her and bring her down. What do you think, Cecilia?'

'I'm thinking of sticking two fingers up at you,' she said. 'You know I'm frightened of German Shepherds. And I'm sure I'm terrified of police dogs. Can't I go indoors and watch through the window?'

It was then it struck me that Charlie seemed unusually subdued.

'You haven't even told us his name,' I said to Charlie.

'Barrie! Will you stop hectoring the poor man!' said Dorothy.

'He asks more questions than CID,' said Charlie.

'OK,' I said, folding my arms. 'I won't ask any more.'

Charlie turned to Dorothy, 'He's like a big kid, your husband, isn't he? I never even got to finish me cup of tea.'

'Go and get Charlie's tea,' said Dorothy looking at me, 'so he can finish it while we're out here.'

I traipsed off, but stopped in the hall, on the other side of the front door, ears flapping. I was beginning to think there was a bit of a mystery here.

'Are you pleased with him, Charlie?' I heard Dorothy ask. There was a pause and then a noise which puzzled me. I put one eye round the door. Charlie was slowly scraping the gravel on the drive with his foot, staring down, in reflective mood.

'BARRIE! Where's that tea?' Dorothy had spotted me. So I didn't hear Charlie's reply.

By the time I'd retrieved the tea, and following Dorothy's thoughtful lead, found a bag of treats, Charlie had opened the back door of his van. The dog unit vans were kitted out to hold two dogs, the cage divided off into two sections so that each dog had his own space, and to prevent altercations. I'd already asked about this in the past and Charlie had explained that although usually he had only the one working German Shepherd with him, he had also sometimes worked a sniffer dog, a spaniel trained to locate illegal drugs. Now, looking out at us from behind the mesh was one dog, a classic German Shepherd.

'Oh, isn't he handsome, Charlie,' said Dorothy. 'How old is he?'

'He's about two,' said Charlie. I handed him his cold tea. He took it and stood staring at it for a few moments, then shook his head. 'You wouldn't believe it,' he said. 'However long was I looking for a dog? And do you know where I got this one from?'

Dorothy and I shook *our* heads.

'The police!'

'What?' I said, half laughing.

Charlie took a swig of his tea. 'He's a fully trained police dog. And he's a cracker!' With a sudden wide sweep of his arm he threw away the dregs of his tea. Now he was talking about his dog we were beginning to see some of the enthusiasm and energy we associated with Charlie whenever he talked about German Shepherd police dogs. 'An absolute cracker!' He leant over to put his face close to the mesh. 'But you're a right handful, aren't you?' he said to the dog.

He turned to Dorothy and me. 'He's full of it. Absolutely full of it. So what he needed was an experienced handler to make the best use of him.' He straightened up and banged the roof of his van with a fist. 'So they gave him to a novice, didn't they? Been on the job ten minutes, worked on a turkey farm all his life before that. That's probably why the brass let him become a dog handler so soon. Turkeys, dogs, both animals, aren't they?'

Charlie was in full flow now. 'He's a real country turnip. For his own sake they should have given him a nice easy dog.' He put his face up close to the mesh so the tip of his nose poked through and he addressed the dog again. 'And you gave the poor devil the time of his life, didn't you?'

He straightened up again, and turned to Dorothy and me. He shook his head again.

'And then they were gonna chuck him off the unit.'

I looked across at Dorothy. I think neither of us were sure whether it was the new handler or the new dog that was to be thrown off the dog unit.

'I had a hell of fight – but in the end I made them let me take him.'

Then Charlie did something utterly unexpected.

He shut the doors of the van.

He turned and walked towards the house. I stood open-mouthed. I looked across at Dorothy. She looked at me and raised her eyebrows.

'Charlie! Aren't we going to meet him?' I called out.

Charlie came to a halt. 'He's got one or two problems – I'd rather sort them first.'

Cecilia took a couple of steps backwards, nearer to the front door.

I wanted to argue with Charlie. I wanted to say, 'You said he was a trained police dog, so you must have him under control.' I think Charlie must have read my thoughts.

'Not all police dogs are Rin Tin Tin, you know,' he said. He strode across to me. 'Dickie on our unit, his dog don't like the dark – don't want to get out of the van if it isn't broad daylight. And one sniff of a bitch on heat and our sergeant's dog is off like a rocket, gone – he can call him till he's got a blue face to match his blue uniform.' He paused. 'They're dogs,' he said with emphasis, 'they're not robots.'

We all fell silent for a couple of moments.

'Well we'll see him another time,' said Dorothy, in placatory mode.

'No, no. Of course you want to meet him,' said Charlie. He pulled open the van doors. 'But he'd rather bite someone than not bite them, that's all.'

He paused before sliding the bolt across on the door of the cage. I suspected he wanted to see if that last piece of information had had the necessary effect.

By the look on Cecilia's face it had certainly had the necessary effect on her, any inclination she had to meet a police dog having entirely vanished.

And as for me, I thought that perhaps it would be more sensible if we postponed meeting the dog until Charlie had had time for further training.

But the look of disappointment on Dorothy's face was more than Charlie could bear. Slowly he slid the bolt across.

In the time I had known Charlie he had struck me as one of life's easy-going individuals, plumpish and placid, usually relaxed. But there was nothing relaxed about him now. His mouth was shut tight, his lips making just a thin line on his face and he was tensed, ready to spring.

He pulled the door open and stood aside to let the dog leap out. At that point I only had a side view of him but I had the impression for a moment that Charlie closed his eyes.

The big dog landed on the ground, paused, looked around, first at me, then at Cecilia, then at Dorothy.

Then he bounded off across the drive and leapt up at Dorothy. He licked her face. Then he dropped down onto all fours, turned sideways and leant against her. Dorothy smiled and patted him two or three times.

Then he trotted over to me and did it all again. As he leant against me, I stroked him and he looked across at Cecilia but made no movement towards her.

Charlie, leaning against the van, was shaking his head slowly.

'You all right, Charlie?' I asked.

'Oh yes,' he said, putting his hand to his forehead, 'never better.'

'You still haven't told us his name,' I said.

'Ivor,' said Charlie. 'Ivor the Terrible.'

At the sound of Charlie's voice, Ivor the Terrible wagged his tail. Then he pushed himself harder against my legs, such that he lost his footing and slid down onto the drive. He raised one front leg and one back leg up in the air, exposing his tummy, to be tickled perhaps.

I looked across at Charlie. He was staring at the ground, still slowly shaking his head.

'What is the matter, Charlie?' I called out.

He looked up at me.

'How do they know?' he said. 'How do they know?'

Hard

I woke early that morning. About six o'clock. It was going to be a special day. It was going to be fulfilling, and make me so happy. It was also going to be hard to get through and leave me feeling hollow.

That's what this rescue work is like. You get pulled in two different directions. It's a real mix of emotions.

For the dog you have found a home for you're relieved and happy that he is no longer homeless. And you have a feeling of satisfaction that you've done all you can to ensure it will be a caring home. But then you feel the sense of responsibility, the weight of it, afraid that you will make a mistake, put him with people where he will repeat what he has been through before.

And the worst part? That comes after you've put him in their car for the new owners. Often, because they have had a dog before, it's an estate car. You shut the door on him. His new people get in the car. It's then you see the first signs of concern on his face: you're not getting in the car with him.

Often you get a hug from the new owners, sometimes even a kiss. And usually words of reassurance: 'Don't worry, we'll look after him.' They'll ring in a few days to let us know how he is settling in.

The turn of the ignition key bringing the engine to life cranks up the anxiety on the dog's face. Now he's restless in the back – he knows that car is going to move off. And it's going to take him with it. But we're not in the car with him.

Our drive is on a slight incline. The people's car goes slowly up the drive, taking what has become our dog away from us. Always, he looks out of the window, staring back at us. What is happening? Who are these people? Where am I going? Why are you sending me away? You are the people who cared for me – why are you now sending me off?

The car turns out of the gate and travels along the village street, usually a hand or an arm projecting from the window, waving back at us.

We watch the car disappear out of sight in the distance. Then we stand for a few moments with our thoughts. Then some encouraging comment or other. 'He was happy to jump in their car, wasn't he?' or 'He was pleased to see them again, wasn't he?' or 'They're lovely people – their vet spoke highly of them.'

But usually we've met them only two or three times before. Strangers who we had to judge. People we had to trust with one of our homeless dogs. People we had to believe when they said they would look after him.

'You're the most difficult people in the world to get a dog from,' we were told by a vet – not our Melissa. He had sent some people to us he thought would provide a good enough home, but we didn't. He meant it as a criticism – we took it as a compliment. 'We don't want to just find a home for the dog,' we would say to prospective owners at our first meeting. 'We want to match the home to the dog and the dog to the home: a home that suits the dog and a dog that suits the home.'

Charlie had been there at one of our meetings. 'You're like a dating agency,' he said.

That made me smile at the time, but afterwards, when I thought about it, I felt he was right, although Dorothy said that in the type of homes we place the dogs with, they became part of the family, so we were more like an adoption agency.

We wanted something for our dogs, a home, but we had to recognise that for the people coming to us we also had something that they wanted: a dog. Young Mr Frank and his live-in girlfriend felt they had room for a big dog as their house had a garden 300 yards long. I decided to drive round there to have a look. Mr Frank was prone to exaggeration in his eagerness to acquire a pedigree German Shepherd dog: his house was on the seventh floor of a block of flats. And Miss Turpin lived alone and wanted a dog as a companion. Her local dog warden said she had four kids under five and their last dog had a ballpoint pen pushed in his ear by one of them.

Today we were to roll the dice again for one of our dogs and hand him over to his new home. And this time it was to be after all the hours spent sitting with him, after all the bathing of his wounds, after all the visits to the vet, making sure he'd had all his tablets, the agonising slow progress, the gradual covering of the hips and the backbone and the ribs with a thin layer of flesh. This time, after all those months, it was to be Friend we sent away up the drive.

We hadn't seen Charlie for weeks and then he turned up two days running.

Although from time to time I would see on the roads other white vans bearing the words POLICE DOG UNIT, there was no mistaking Charlie's van. Winter in our locality saw tractors and huge trailers carting potatoes and sugar beet off the fields, the massive tractor wheels scattering mud on the rural roads for cars to spray on to one another. It wasn't somewhere to live if you liked your car to be always clean and shiny. Dorothy and I thought a muddy look suited our old Volvo estate, and Charlie obviously felt the same about his dog van. When he pulled up on the drive today, the lawyer in me noticed that his rear number plate was obscured with mud, contrary to the road traffic regulations. But then Charlie never struck me as the sort of policeman who was hot on motoring offences. In any case, when he got out of his van he didn't look to be in his bonniest mood, so I decided not to wind him up about the offence he was committing. His frowning face prompted me to ask immediately if I should put the kettle on.

'They dragged me all the way over to some place I'd never heard of – 30 miles when it's chucking it down with rain – and it's a total waste of time.' He slammed the door of his van. 'It's a break-in – the lad had run off and they want Ivor to follow his trail. How can he follow his trail when they've put their big boots all over it?' He coughed a couple of times then took out his packet of Golden Virginia.

'Got Ivor with you?' I asked.

He ignored the question. 'You was gonna tell me yesterday where Digby had gone.'

'I forgot, didn't I, in the excitement of meeting Ivor.'

It had been remiss of me not to make the effort to keep him in the picture about Digby. Not only had Charlie willingly presided at our first naming ceremony but our ex-guard dog from a car breakers' yard had been named in memory of a particular police dog.

I made up for the omission with tea and chocolate digestives, seated round the fire.

'He went to someone not too far removed from your line of work. In fact, he takes over where you and Ivor leave off.'

'Works in hospital, does he?'

The joke made me smile. It also brought back to mind what Charlie had said yesterday about Ivor preferring to bite someone rather than not biting them.

'Do you want that last biscuit?' Charlie asked.

I shook my head.

'I was on tenterhooks yesterday about getting him out because the brass is afraid all the time of getting sued, you see,' said Charlie. 'Although what's putting the wind up them most about my lad is when he runs after and catches a villain who's legged it. Once I set him on after some bloke, that's it.'

'Brilliant.'

'Yes, but once he's got hold of 'em when I call him off he goes stone deaf. He will not let go. Don't worry me, but it worries my Inspector.'

I could see that would worry his Inspector.

'And he likes to chew 'em up a bit.'

I could see that that would worry his Inspector even more.

'And today, of course, any excuse and they'll sue. Anyway...' Charlie paused to suck the end of a finger and use it to pick up biscuit crumbs which had dropped onto his tunic. '... Digby?'

'Digby was adopted by a guy who works in a prison. He's rung me loads of times since. He idolises the dog, he absolutely idolises the dog.'

'So he should,' said Charlie. 'Terrific dog.'

'He starts work at six o'clock in the morning and he gets up at half-four to give Digby a walk before he goes to work.'

'Good man.'

'Of course at weekends Digby still expects to go for a walk at half past four in the morning.'

'Well he would.'

'Yes, but he pulls the bedclothes off the bloke.'

'I knew that was a bright dog,' said Charlie. He stood up.

'You off?'

'That was Dorothy's motor I just heard on the drive, wasn't it?'

'Yes, but you don't have to run off because—'

'No! I've got something to show you – I've been waiting for her to come home. Out in the van. That van's got two dog compartments, remember?'

And that was how Millie came to us.

I took a photo of Millie that day she came in, standing in the middle of the lawn. When I showed the photo to people what they saw was a classic German Shepherd female: black and tan, pointed ears, alert expression.

And Millie liked to pose. For the photo she had adopted the 'Shepherd stand'. Owners and breeders who compete with German Shepherds at shows hope their dog will impress the judge by standing with one back leg extended beyond the other. So any devotee of German Shepherds who viewed the photo was full of admiration for the beautiful female depicted.

But really the photo revealed what a failed photographer I was. It didn't show Millie's most striking – and astonishing – characteristic: her size. Nothing in the photo indicated that Millie was the tiniest German Shepherd I or anybody I knew had ever seen. The perfect German Shepherd in every way, with all the personality traits of the breed: intelligence, eagerness to learn, wanting to be with you, and a guard. But a very, very small guard.

'Some people rang into the office and offered us a German Shepherd they didn't want any more. The sergeant sent me along to have a look and I nearly threw up. Barrie, the place – it stunk. It absolutely stunk.'

'Do you think she's a runt of the litter?' I asked.

'I don't like that word,' said Dorothy. 'She's small but perfectly formed. And Millie's got an advantage over other German Shepherds.' She squatted down, wrapped her arms around Millie and scooped her up. She stood up smiling broadly. 'You can pick her up and cuddle her!'

Charlie opened the door of his van. 'Couldn't leave her there, could I? So I told 'em we'd take her. They were as thick as I don't know what. Fed her on table scraps.' He pointed at her. 'No wonder she's so thin.

She was eating tomato skins when I got there.' He got into his van.

'Charlie, do I take it that you're leaving her with us?'

'Yeah, but of course they don't know that. They think she's gonna be a police dog. They want me to send a photo of her at the Passing Out Parade. If I took her back to the Unit and said I was gonna spend £10,000 training her as a police dog it would be my Inspector who passed out.'

I went into the utility room, closed the door behind me and sat down on the floor.

'I've got something to tell you, Friend. That really nice young woman you met the other day... you're going to go with her today. And you're going to live with her for the rest of your life.

'You and I have spent a lot of hours together in this utility room, haven't we? I've come to quite like sitting on the floor.

'Because I love you so much I can't be here when you leave. I don't want to see you go up that drive, giving me that look that says, Why are you sending me away? Hannah will care for you and love you like I do. And she'll be able to give you the time I can't.

'This is your big day. It's the start of your new life.

'God bless you. I'm going to go now.'

The Christmas Present

'Hello, I do hope you can help. My husband's a self-employed builder. He went into a house to do some repairs and there was a dog there.'

I already had enough experience of such phone calls to speculate on what this morning's caller had done next. The people said they didn't want it any more and gave it to him? Or the dog was neglected and her husband took it away from them?

'I think it's an Alsatian – but you don't call them that now, do you? Neither of us know much about dogs – we haven't got one, but I think it's an old dog.'

I took a deep breath. I had learnt by now that the problem with taking a dog from people to whom it didn't belong was that they would know hardly anything about the dog or, more likely, nothing at all.

'He seems ever so friendly but, bless him, he doesn't walk right. He doesn't go in a straight line, if you know what I mean. But of course we didn't know this until we'd untied him.'

'You untied him?'

'Yes, he was tied up. I don't recognise the code for your number and I think you must be a long way away but we're hoping you'll take him from us. We can't possibly keep him, although I've already started to get attached to him and we've only had him two days.'

'Did the people you got him from tell you anything about him?'

There were several seconds of silence at the other end of the phone.

'I've just realised I've explained this badly. There was nobody there. The people had moved out three days before.'

'Is that the place that takes in dogs?' began my second caller of the day.

'Er, yes.'

'My boyfriend give me a dog and I don't want it – will you take it?'

Struggling to hear what the girl was saying, I pressed the phone hard against my ear. In the background I could make out the sound of young children shouting and screaming and adverts on the telly.

'Er... can you tell me a bit about it, please?'

'He's give it to me as a Christmas present – I don't want a dog. I've got enough to do with two kids.'

'Do you know what breed it is? Do you know how old it is?'

'There ain't any papers with it but it looks like an Alsatian. It's only little so it's not very old. He got it from his mate. I could bring it tonight if you can take it.'

I sighed. The old boy found tied up in the empty house was on his way to me right now and she wants me to take this one tonight... And it's Christmas next week – not a good time to be trying to find a home for a dog.

'STOP IT! LEAVE IT ALONE!'

I nearly dropped the phone.

'Sorry about that – the kids are driving me mad. The dog keeps taking their toys and playing with them! It's doing my head in!'

I sighed again. Christmas or no Christmas, perhaps we should take a second dog today.

The phone was ringing again, minutes later.

'Hello!' I heard from a voice full of enthusiasm. 'I hope I've got the right number. My friend says you're the people who rescue pooches.'

'Er... yes.'

'Can I come and see them?'

'Well that's not actually how we work. If you'd like to tell me what it is you're looking for—'

'The younger the better! Help me lose some of this weight!'

The younger the better? Hmmm.

'Well, we may be able to help you. If I may ask some questions first...'

I didn't hear the car on the drive at the front. I was standing at the back door. My ears were fully occupied listening to the barking coming from down at the pens.

It seemed to me it had been going on for a long, long time though in fact it was probably only twenty minutes. I've never complained about other people's barking dogs but I have every sympathy with anyone who finds it an agitating distraction. Our dog barking – it sounded as if it was Millie – had gone on long enough to have me thinking about taking an extra blood pressure tablet. A complaint to the local dog warden from one of our neighbours and we might end up with our transit camp shut down.

This prolonged barking happened from time to time and was a recurring source of anxiety for me. I'd have to go down there in the dark and see what was the matter. But I couldn't go just yet – there was somebody banging at the front door.

The woman on the phone that morning with the unwanted Christmas present had said she would come this evening. Presumably this was her. I pulled open the front door to find two women standing with their backs to me. Hearing the door open, one turned round.

'Is this Happy Cottage?'

I nodded and smiled. It always made me smile when I heard other people use the name Dorothy had given our little house.

The other woman turned round. She wore a furry overcoat and either had an enormous chest or had something stuffed inside her coat. She stepped forward into the porch light and I could see two little eyes looking out at me from inside the coat.

'We was watching the car,' said the first woman. 'Your drive's slopey and the handbrake don't work on my car.'

The second woman put her hand inside her coat and pulled out a little furry thing that grunted as it met the December night air. She put her other hand underneath it to support it then turned it round for me to see it. It was all dark fur apart from a small area of pink belly.

'We can't stop,' said the second woman. 'My mate's got to get back to her kids.' She held out her arms for me to take the puppy. As I put my hands around it, it grunted again. I held it against my chest trying to cover it from the cold night air with my hands.

'Me boyfriend says he was told she's about five weeks old.'

I shook my head. I was about to say that the pup should still be with his mother – but what was the point?

The woman turned to go.

'Hang on! You haven't told me her name!'

She looked round. 'Sniffy.'

'Sniffy?'

'Cos it sniffs at everything.' She turned to go again.

'Did you bring anything with you for her? Anything she's familiar with – has she got a bed? Or her toys?'

'I forgot its blanket. Toys? I didn't give it any toys.' She pulled a face indicating surprised disbelief. 'I've never had a dog – do you give 'em toys?'

So now we knew why this baby was playing with the human baby's toys.

After a hurried goodbye the pair were gone.

I closed the front door and stood in the hallway, clutching this little bundle of life to my chest. I shook my head in bewilderment. For me, every dog that comes to us is precious and special – we've never had one that was the same as another. I'm left with a sense of wonder that to some people a dog means nothing, that they can discard them without a thought or a look back. They give us something which to them has no worth or use – yet to me is priceless.

And now a puppy. A baby, with all her life ahead of her. With the promise of all that companionship and love and fun to come. Discarded in a hurry.

My thoughts were interrupted by the realisation that something was nibbling the end of my finger. I sighed: no puppy food. And of course her owner hadn't thought to bring any – but then they've probably been feeding her on chips. Good job the supermarket stayed open late tonight.

Dorothy was in the loft looking for the Christmas decorations. I went and stood at the bottom of the loft ladder.

'Dorotheeeeee!'

'I'm up here!' said a voice. 'I'm trying to find the crackers we had left from last year. I'll be down in a minute.'

I looked down at the soft warm bundle cradled in my arms. Then I looked up into the hole above my head.

'If you saw what I've got down here,' I said, 'You wouldn't bother with those old crackers.'

Dorothy had needed something to cheer her up. Me too.

The day had brought us two German Shepherd dogs: one at the start of her life and one at the other end.

We felt we had to change the name of the dog who had been tied to a banister when his owners moved out. With no name tag on his collar, the concerned woman who had brought him to us had called him Pepper.

She had taken inspiration from a soft drink can she had found in her husband's van. Pepper seemed to us perhaps more suitable for a smaller breed of dog, or one livelier than this dog.

Still fresh in our minds was a story Charlie had told us recently about a police dog he had known. His mate Ginger had arrested a youth in a stolen car. Suddenly there was a knife in the young man's hand and he ran at the officer. Thor jumped between them and took the full force of the knife. So Pepper became Thor.

'We'll have to give Charlie a ring,' I said. 'Get him to come and do one of his naming ceremonies.'

Dorothy was watching Thor as he made slow progress round the garden.

She compressed her lips. 'I think, my Barrie, we wouldn't want Charlie to leave it too long before he came.'

I didn't reply. A feeling of sadness flowed through me.

What sort of life had he had with people who could leave him behind with the rubbish? When a dog comes to us whose life is nearly over, and who has had a poor quality of life – that is what I find demoralising. With the younger dog, the wrong could mostly be put right, and he still has time to live the life he should have. We need to put out of our thoughts past lack of care, callousness, brutality, and work for the future, and that's how you energise and motivate yourself. But how do you motivate yourself with the dog who comes to you at the end of his life?

Somehow. Because you have to put him right and you have to find him a home. Even if that home is only for a few weeks. Then at least he will end his days with people who care about him and look after him.

All this was in my thoughts as we watched Thor. I could see why the kindly woman who had brought him to us, Mrs Duxford, had said he could not walk in a straight line. His back right leg pointed inwards, the paw of his left back leg was folded under and dragged along the ground as he walked. The cumulative effect for him was that as he walked forward he would gradually veer off to the left. His body was that which is often seen with the very elderly dog: gaunt. Here and there were sores where we guessed he had spent too many hours lying down.

We had made it a practice to take a photo of each dog on the day he left to go to his new home so I was surprised when Dorothy said, 'I should go and get the camera, Barrie, and take his picture now.'

I framed the photo carefully. It is a picture only of Thor's head. For whatever time and neglect had done to the rest of him he had still the classic head of the German Shepherd. And not just any German Shepherd: his head was bigger than average and he was still handsome.

Dorothy was better at guessing ages than I was. 'How old do you think he is?' I asked her.

'It's not easy to say, really,' she said. 'As with people, neglect hastens the ageing process. But I would guess he's around twelve. He must have been a terrific dog in his prime. Even now, look how tall his shoulders stand from the ground. And that broad chest.'

My photo shows a handsome male German Shepherd looking up at the camera, alert and bright-eyed, ears erect. The picture captured in his face the essence of him – you didn't need to see the rest.

At our usually busy vet's Dorothy, Thor and I had the waiting room to ourselves. Only another couple of days and it would be Christmas Eve. It was Saturday afternoon and everybody was probably shopping or busy with their Christmas preparations.

We were glad we had the waiting room to ourselves, for it was a restless German Shepherd dog we had brought to see the vet. Up and down the waiting room he struggled at the end of his lead, panting, coming back at short intervals to nudge one of us for a reassuring stroke of the head.

I hadn't got my eyes on him when he fell to the floor. So I didn't see what had happened. We jumped up from our chairs but before we could kneel down to help him up he was scrambling and slithering to his feet. And I hadn't seen Melissa standing at the open door of the consulting room.

'I've been watching him,' she said.

I could see the concern in her face.

'How often does he fall?' she asked.

'It's the first time we've seen it,' said Dorothy, 'but he only came to us this afternoon and we haven't walked him any distance, just a little way round the garden and from the car to here.'

'Come through,' said Melissa.

We were back in the waiting room. We must have been with Melissa for nearly an hour. Thor had submitted without complaint to pulling, rubbing, pushing, prodding by this stranger. Now Melissa had gone off with some blood samples to test.

'Did you see the dog before you agreed to take him?' she had asked us.

We had both shaken our heads.

While I sat on the hard waiting room chair her question came back into my mind. I had time to think about why she asked it. If we had seen him would we still have taken him?

Melissa reappeared, forced a smile, and sat down beside me. His visit to the vet had tired him and Thor was sitting on his haunches, slumped against me. Sitting down was for him a slow process, his back end going down gingerly to the floor. Melissa gazed admiringly at that big Shepherd head.

'He must have been a magnificent specimen in his prime,' she said. Then she leant forward and tickled his ear. 'Weren't you, Thor?' she said to him.

'So where do we stand, Melissa?' said Dorothy.

Melissa ceased to tickle the boy's ear. 'Really hard to say,' said Melissa. 'A few weeks, perhaps.'

Several seconds of silence followed.

Then, outside, in the street, a group of carol singers began to sing 'Silent night'. I turned and through the window could see the group, two of their number shaking buckets at passers-by in the pub car park opposite.

Christmas. It wasn't so long after Christmas that it would be our wedding anniversary. And that meant it would be one year that we had been doing this work, taking in homeless dogs. I suppose it was inevitable that one day we would take in the dog we could not home.

I turned away from gazing out at the carol singers and the Christmas shoppers jostling on the pavement. My eyes met Dorothy's. Was this going to be the dog that ended his days not with a family of his own but in a dog sanctuary? The dog that was discarded, that did not have his own person? For him, no home of his own? The carol singers upped their volume and 'Silent night, holy night' swirled round the waiting room.

'It's a beautiful carol, isn't it,' said Melissa. She stood up. 'If a prospective owner wants to speak to me about his condition I'd be happy to do so, of course.'

Dorothy looked up at her. 'Thanks. But we've got to be realistic... somebody taking on a dog with only a few weeks to...? And there would be the vet bills.'

Melissa nodded. Her brow furrowed, the concern she shared with us plain to see.

I sensed she wanted to speak, but was hesitating.

'Did you want me to—' she said after several moments.

'Not unless he's in pain,' Dorothy said quickly and firmly.

'No, I'm sure with the injection and painkillers he'll be quite comfortable. Except if he falls he could injure himself, of course.'

'That's the only time we've seen him fall over,' I said. 'And it is a slippery floor in here, with the tiles.'

Melissa nodded. 'I'll just go and see to that prescription,' she said.

The carol singers had moved away and we found ourselves sitting again in silence.

I broke the silence by saying, 'One of us could adopt him.'

214

'It wouldn't be the same,' said Dorothy. 'In reality it would just be a gesture. We would be doing it because he hadn't really got someone of his own. It's a nice thought, Barrie, but it isn't actually the answer.'

I counted the boxes of tablets as Melissa put them on the counter: one, two, three, four, five.

We wished Melissa a merry Christmas and trudged off with our old boy who could not walk in a straight line, having to make our way to our car through the bustling crowds of Christmas shoppers.

Driving home, I made the effort to sound cheerful, to talk of the things I knew Dorothy liked about Christmas.

'We could go and get a tree and decorate it tonight,' I said, trying to sound enthusiastic. 'Thor could help us.'

Dorothy managed a smile.

'And we've got those new lights we bought last year – they're so pretty.'

'There's somebody standing in our porch,' said Dorothy as we pulled onto the drive. We had been so long at the vet's I had forgotten about the prospective owner that had rung that morning.

'It might be the lady who's come to see the puppy – but she's very early.' That wasn't a complaint – we both liked it when prospective owners arrived early. We thought it showed their enthusiasm. We had had the puppy only a couple of days but at just five weeks old and too young to have left her mother, she needed lots of care. The sooner we found a home that could give her all the attention and time she needed, the better.

'This is a bright dog,' had been Dorothy's assessment of her. 'She learns quickly.'

And she was very inquisitive, wanting to inspect everything, also a sign of her German Shepherd intelligence. When she saw Thor for the first time she ran away and hid behind Dorothy's leg, but even then her sense of curiosity overcame her and she kept peeping out to look at this huge creature.

The figure left the porch and came across to greet us. 'Hello, I'm Doreen. I've come to see the pup. Oh, and to be vetted, of course.'

Dorothy and I introduced ourselves, Doreen shaking each of our hands vigorously.

'I'm so pleased to meet you and I'm so excited.'

I said I was pleased to meet her – and I was, too. Her cheerful enthusiasm was medicine for our depleted spirits.

'Oh I do love a real fire,' she exclaimed when we went through into the living room. 'I'm sorry if I'm early. I sat at home with my hat and coat on for a while but then I just couldn't contain myself any longer.'

Over tea and chocolate digestives Doreen told us her life story. We didn't have to go through the usual question and answer session. It was over a year since her last dog had died and it had taken her until now before she felt she could have another.

'I know some people can go and get another dog the next day, but I just couldn't,' she said. 'I needed time to grieve – I don't know if that sounds silly.'

Not to us it didn't.

She ran her own smallholding, mostly growing fruit and vegetables, with a few free-range chickens.

216

'So she'll have plenty of room to run about for exercise – there's eight acres – although of course I'll take her out for walks every day. Because I've got land for her to run about, that's one reason why I want a young one.'

'Well,' I said, 'we've certainly got a young one...'

Doreen towered above Dorothy and me, and was heavily built; I guessed that her smallholding work had helped to develop her big arms. Cradled in those arms, the puppy looked even smaller than before.

'Oh, she's utterly gorgeous. What's her name?'

Like Thor, she had undergone a name change. Sniffy had now become Bliss.

Dorothy had of course bought from the pet shop an assortment of toys and we watched as Doreen lay on the floor, immersed in the joys of playing with a puppy.

I was thinking that time was getting on and we had dogs to walk when Doreen said, 'I'm taking up so much of your time. But it's a long while since I did this. My last girl was ten when she died – and ten weeks when I got her.'

She left Bliss and sat down on the settee, gazing at the fire. Dorothy and I looked at one another. The bounce seemed to have gone out of Doreen.

'Would you like another cup of tea?' Dorothy offered.

Doreen shook her head. 'I'm sorry,' she said, 'but it brings back too many memories. She's just so like my old dog, Chrissie.'

She suddenly stood up. 'I've made a mistake – I can't have another puppy.' She looked at me and then at Dorothy. 'I'm so sorry I've wasted your time.'

She took out a handkerchief, blew her nose, and hurried out.

It must have been a couple of hours later that I heard a tapping on the living room window. I'd had time since Doreen left to walk Lottie, the Lurcher, and feed the others, Larry, the brown Labrador cross, tiny Millie, Thor and Bliss. The nights drawing in so early made it seem later than it really was and it was a surprise to see the clock in the hall tell me it was only eight o'clock. I opened the front door and was about to step out to see who was at the window when I stopped myself just in time, to avoid colliding with a Christmas tree. A Christmas tree that was taller than me.

Doreen appeared out of the darkness.

'I heard you say you hadn't got your Christmas tree yet, and you always have a real one, so I've brought you this one.'

Dorothy appeared beside me.

'Did you hear that?' I said. Her mouth was open in astonishment.

'It's a wonderful tree,' she said. 'I can't normally afford one as nice as this.'

'No. We normally end up with some straggly thing,' I said, 'that we get on Christmas Eve.'

I leant round the tree. 'But Doreen, what's this for – why have you brought us this?'

'My uncle grows them and I sell a few for him as part of my farm-gate sales. I felt so guilty at having wasted your time I wanted to get you something to say sorry.'

'Oh, how lovely!' said Dorothy. 'And how kind.'

'We both love having a real Christmas tree,' I said.

'You must have so much pressure on your time, helping these dogs,' said Doreen, 'and I felt awful afterwards at wasting it. I'll help you carry it in, if you like.'

I took one side of the pot and Doreen the other. It took some lifting and manoeuvring to get it through the door.

'Dorothy and I needed this to cheer us up,' I said to Doreen as I shuffled backwards.

'Why is that, my darlings?' she said.

Dorothy pushed open the living room door. Through the open door Thor could be seen lying stretched out in front of the fire. Dragging the pot down the hall I paused. 'We'll tell you about it over a Christmas drink. It's that lad, there,' I said, nodding in the direction of the dog sprawled out on the fireside rug.

'Oh bless him,' said Doreen. 'What's wrong with him?'

'What's right with him?' I said.

She left me grappling with the tree, went to Thor and stood gazing down at him. He lifted his head from the rug, looked up at her for several moments, then managed a wag of his tail.

It was love at first sight for them both.

Christmases since then always make me think about Doreen and her Thor. There was much to think about.

This woman had come to us for a young dog yet she had given a home to an old-age pensioner. We can all of us make seemingly rational judgements about what dog would suit us and our home – but in reality our emotions are our boss. In the comparatively short space of time Thor was with Doreen he brought immense pleasure into her life, and when the day came that she had to say goodbye to him she told us, 'He was the greatest dog I've ever known. He was such a character. I loved him dearly.' And it was her act of kindness, coming back to give us a Christmas tree, that caused Thor to come into her life.

Perhaps Thor had never before known a loving, caring home, for how else do we explain his rejuvenation? Or perhaps it was the herbal remedy Doreen gave him. Or the friendship he struck up with Lucky, her cat. So for once, just once, Melissa was wrong: it wasn't just weeks. He made it through the winter, enjoyed the spring and was fortunate to experience one of those glorious English summers we have from time to time, when he could be seen sprawled out under his favourite tree, Lucky beside him, sunbathing.

He died in his sleep, under that tree, in late autumn.

He had given Doreen companionship, laughter and even a little exercise throwing his ball for him. She had given him some life.

And she had given us not only a Christmas tree but the present of a home for Thor. It had been the best Christmas present we could have had.

A Perfect Match

The two men opened the back doors of the truck. Along either side of the interior was a row of built-in cages. Two or three of the cages were empty but in each of the others, some seven or eight, a dog looked out at us.

I looked down the rows.

'Yours isn't in those,' said one of the men. 'We'd have to let him out if he was.' He clambered into the truck and went to the back where I could make out in the gloomy interior a free-standing cage on the floor. As he dragged it forward I could see the Shepherd inside. At the doors of the truck the man paused for us to get a look at the dog in daylight. He sat on his hindquarters, his head lowered, taking no interest in us, his eyes glazed, staring vacantly ahead of him. He made the effort to stand on all fours but his back legs wouldn't support him and he slipped down.

Some of the other dogs were barking, some whining, some silent.

'Where are all these others going?' I asked the man in the wagon. He was the older of the two and I surmised the younger man with him was his assistant.

'A bloke at Yarborough,' said the older man. 'When he can, he takes some of the seven-dayers.' He jumped down out of the wagon.

'Seven-dayers?'

'Under our contract with the council, at the end of the seven days we can dispose of them. If it's an old one, or it's sick, we're not likely to home them. Usually we only destroy the others if we're full.'

'But we're nearly always full,' said the young man.

The older man tapped the cage with his finger. 'This one would have had to go, as he's a biter. He would have gone weeks ago if it wasn't that they were hoping to prosecute.' He ran his fingers backwards and forwards across the bars of the cage. The dog tilted his head a little to one side in an effort to see what the man was doing. 'I think he's starting to come out of this – we need to get him out of the cage and into wherever you want him quick. I assume you've got somewhere nice and secure for him.'

'We've been told he can be a bit aggressive,' I said.

'He'll have you,' said the man. He looked at his young assistant. 'That reminds me – don't let me go, Lee, without giving him the paperwork.' He looked at me. 'You'll have to sign our lawyer stuff that absolves us from all legal liability for what the dog does to you.'

Dorothy had been at work when the two men brought our latest arrival, so naturally as soon as she got home she had hurried off down to the pen to see him. I explained that the dog pound had given him some stuff to sedate him.

'Presumably he doesn't travel well, then, if they've had to sedate him for the journey,' said Dorothy.

Hmm. I doubted whether it was for the journey that the men had sedated him. They had carried the cage into the pen, upended it to tip the dog out, and were then in such a hurry to get out of the pen that they collided at the door. Not that the dog looked to be any sort of a threat. He stood in the middle of the pen, a dreamy look on his face, swaying slightly – how I looked after two glasses of wine. I'd decided to leave him for a few hours to recover and acclimatise himself to his new surroundings.

As we approached the pen now we could see him lying close to the door, curled up.

'What's his name?' asked Dorothy.

'They called him Growler at the dog pound,' I said.

Dorothy pulled a face. 'We can't call him that.'

I'd been watching the telly when Dorothy got home – a repeat of one of my favourite shows of all time, *The Dukes of Hazzard*. I usually found it hard to come up with names for the dogs but today I had a source of inspiration.

'What about Bo?' I suggested, thinking of one of the lead characters in the show.

Dorothy's expression indicated that she was not impressed. We were at the pen now and the dog remained curled up but looking at us, eyeing us suspiciously I thought.

'What about Denver?' I said after the actor who played my favourite character.

Dorothy knelt down to talk to the dog. 'I think,' she said to him through the wire mesh, 'that we ought to get to know you a bit better so we can find something suitable.'

'Or what about Rosco?' I said. 'He's the Sheriff.'

'Yes, I know,' Dorothy said.

I dropped down on my knees beside her. The dog leapt to his feet so suddenly and with such alacrity it made me jump and I toppled over backwards. He erupted into a frenzy of furious barking, his lips turned back as far as he could manage, to show his teeth, his jaws snapping shut, his eyes wide. Even Dorothy was momentarily taken aback.

I scrambled up. The dog flung himself at the wire mesh, tilted his head and grabbed the wire with his teeth, tugging it to get at me. Despite the strong wire between me and the dog I took two or three steps backwards.

Dorothy got slowly to her feet and also stepped back from the wire.

'Goodness,' I said, 'I wasn't expecting that.' I could feel my heart beating from the unpleasant jolt.

The dog let go of the wire, spun round in a circle, then grabbed it again.

'Let's move away,' said Dorothy. 'He's getting himself in a frenzy.'

We walked off a few yards to watch him at a distance. But neither the barking nor the pulling at the wire subsided.

'We'll have to leave him for now,' said Dorothy. She turned and set off back to the house.

I stayed for a few moments, watching the spectacle of this dog snarling and barking and frantically clawing at the wire.

I followed after Dorothy. 'Whatever are we going to do with him?' I said.

'For now, all we can do is leave him to calm down,' said Dorothy. 'Tell me more about what we know of him.'

What we knew of him had come via Cecilia, who knew somebody who did rescue work, who knew somebody who did rescue work, who knew about this dog. Taking a dog that came through Cecilia always had an element of uncertainty: you couldn't know what you were getting until it arrived. But it was so difficult to say no to Cecilia, plus she had found us an A-starred home for Bliss the pup with a retired RAF police dog handler.

The manager of the pound had told us that a man, tall and heavily built, had been seen by some people to pick the dog up and throw him into the road in front of a bus as it moved off. Mercifully, the bus driver had swerved and somehow missed the dog. The man was never identified and the dog had no name tag.

Dorothy was unusually quiet for the next couple of hours. She was immersed in a book for much of the time, which wasn't unusual, but every now and then she would look up and gaze at the fire.

I watched as she closed her book, went to the cupboard where we kept the clean food dishes and filled one with a couple of mugfuls of the dry dog food that we used. I guessed who it was for and that we would be off shortly down to that pen, and that she had, by now, formulated a plan of action for us and the dog.

She put on her dog-walking jacket, and picked up the food bowl, then went back into the living room and picked up her book. Bowl in one hand and book in the other, she went to the back door. She paused. My puzzlement must have clearly shown on my face.

'I'm going to go and sit with him,' she said.

My puzzled expression must have turned into a surprised one.

'If I just sit there, he'll get used to me. I'll go and sit with him every day for a few hours. They're an intelligent breed – he'll soon realise I'm no threat.'

'Dorothy, you're not going in there with him!'

'No, for today and tomorrow I'll just sit outside. I'll have to go in at some point tomorrow to clean him out—'

'Dorothy, you can't.'

She must have heard the concern in my voice for she put down book and bowl, came to me, put her arms around me and gave me a hug. Then she pointed with her finger at the unseen operation scar under her clothes. 'We had a near-miss with my illness,' she said, 'so I'm not taking any risks – don't worry.'

'But Dorothy you saw what he was like.'

'It was fear, Barrie. He was frightened. I looked into his eyes.'

'Well I can't sit down there for hours but I'll come with you and stay for a bit,' I said.

'I reckon we'll make faster progress if I go on my own,' she said.

'You are joking!'

'He didn't set off barking and snarling until you bobbed down close to him – up to then he'd been all right with me.'

'I hadn't done—'

'It was a man who threw him in front of the bus. And if that was his owner, can you imagine what else he's been through with him?' She went back to the door. 'It's no good arguing, Barrie. I tell you what, if you let me do this my way, I'll agree to call him Bo.'

She picked up her book and bowl and set off down the garden.

After a couple of minutes I followed her and watched from a distance behind a shrub, armed with a broom for self-defence. But it wasn't needed.

The phone was ringing.

'Oh, hello... Are you the gentleman that takes in dogs that need a home?'

Gentleman? 'Yes, we do take in dogs.'

'Um... this might be a waste of your time...'

I hope not.

'I'm thinking of adopting a dog... but I'm not sure about it...'

I was about to say what a huge responsibility it was to take a dog into your family and that you need to be very sure about it.

'... because I've never had a dog before.'

Oh. I could see why that would make somebody unsure.

'Well, we all start somewhere,' I said. 'We all have to have our very first dog.'

'Yes. I hadn't thought of it that way. Who am I speaking to, please?'

'My name's Barrie.'

'My name is Thomas.'

'Well, Thomas, how we normally operate is—'

'It's Mr Thomas.'

'Oh, sorry! I misunderstood.'

'I should mention that I'm not looking for a big dog.'

I was about to say that is all we ever have when I checked myself. After all, down in the pen in the old barn was Lottie, the Lurcher cross. I wouldn't call her a big dog. And indoors was our Labrador cross, Larry, and most people wouldn't call him a big dog. And then there was Millie, who Charlie had brought to us, the World's Smallest German Shepherd.

'Would you like to tell me a little more about yourself, Mr Thomas...?' I said.

Dorothy felt it would be useful for the future if we kept a note of how we handled troubled dogs, the approach we took with different problems and what worked and what didn't work.

With Bo she wrote this in the form of a diary.

DAY ONE: Brought to us heavily sedated. Barking, snarling in pen – fear aggression? Sat outside pen reading book two hours. Ferocious barking at first for some fifteen minutes, tailing off to occasional outbursts if I moved.

DAY TWO: Short burst aggressive barking at first. Sat and read for three hours. After one hour, moved chair close to pen so he could sniff my hand through wire if he wanted to – short outbreak of barking. Look of fear in eyes gone – now tilting head with puzzlement. I think curiosity is going to get the better of him. Had to go in the pen to clear it out. Slowly opened pen door – he backed away, tail between legs. Talked to him every so often in a calm voice – he clearly always listens. Can't say the same about husband!

DAY THREE: Bit of barking as I approached – partly because I think he was dozing and my sudden appearance startled him. Just half an hour sitting reading this time before going into pen. Came back later for second sit with book – very brief wag of the tail when he first spotted me then abruptly stopped, almost as if he checked himself because he shouldn't be wagging his tail. While reading this time I kept my hand up against the mesh. He sniffed it a couple of times then nudged it later. I pulled out my lead and held it up. I am sure I read in his face a mixture of expressions: some eagerness mixed with uncertainty. Opened door of pen: backed off two or three steps, paused, came forward two or three steps. Bobbed down holding out closed hand a little way. He sniffed it to discover a hidden bit of cheese. Took this, then in a minute another, then in a minute another. He is getting used to my hand. Can I now clip the lead on his collar? Yes!

DAY FOUR: Twenty minutes walk this morning, only five minutes yesterday on his first walk as he was looking apprehensive at being away from his now familiar surroundings.

DAY FIVE: Let him off lead? Garden securely fenced, can't get out – but will he come back to me if I call him? No, not yet. I had to go to him. Backed off – a surprise, as didn't back off in pen this morning. He's still not confident.

DAY SIX: Threw ball – looked at me as if I'm demented. Never been played with. Startled by sudden loud motorbike going by. Ran to gate, tried to clamber over

– I didn't want to grab him. Talked quietly and tried to distract him by pretending to find something in grass. Calmed down, but he gave me a fright.

DAY SEVEN: Saw me coming and jumped up at wire, tail wagging. Can't help but think how a week ago this dog was to be euthanised because he was aggressive. If I'd been thrown under a bus, I would be aggressive. He has kind eyes.

I liked Mr Thomas – which was just as well because I would see a lot of him over the next few weeks.

Mr Thomas was a cautious man, which is a commendable quality in a person undertaking the task of identifying, from the thousands of homeless dogs available, one who would be suitable.

'No doubt you have many questions you want to ask me,' said Mr Thomas on our first meeting, crossing his hands in his lap, shoulders back, ready for the cross-examination. And I liked it when he took his reading glasses out of their case and produced from a pocket of his suit jacket a list of questions he wished to put to me. 'As I haven't undertaken dog ownership before,' he explained.

It was a long list. It started with the usual questions. What should I feed this dog? How often should I walk the dog? How long should the walks be? He was obviously a caring person concerned with the welfare of the dog and the quality of its life. It was when we were up to around question number thirty – and I realised that I'd missed *The Dukes of Hazzard* – that I thought it was actually time to meet a dog.

I remarked to Mr Thomas how fortuitous his timing was: that at the moment we had three dogs that might suit him as they weren't the large dogs we usually took in. But Mr Thomas and I had different ideas about what constituted a 'large' dog.

'Goodness – I only have a small house,' he said on meeting Larry, the Labrador cross. 'I'd have to get a bigger car,' was prompted by the sight of Lurcher cross, Lottie. And 'She would need a very big basket to be comfortable and stretch herself out,' was his response to seeing Millie, the World's Smallest German Shepherd.

Now, we never take the view that it is part of our function to persuade a prospective home to take either any dog or any particular dog. We're not in the business of 'selling' our orphans. But if we feel a dog has certain attributes that would make it suitable for the prospective home, then by pointing these out we can help the prospective owner to come to an informed decision. And I had a feeling that Millie would suit Mr Thomas and that Mr Thomas would suit Millie.

'Shall we take her for a short walk?' I suggested.

'Oh yes. In fact I think I would need to come for several walks with a dog so that we were well acquainted with one another before I was to actually make a decision.'

'Look at the dainty way she picks up her feet as she walks,' I pointed out helpfully. Dressed in a suit, I thought at first that Mr Thomas must have come straight from work to our meeting, but it transpired that he was retired and I surmised that he had put on a suit especially for his 'interview'. I suspected that his terraced house would prove to be as neat as Mr

Thomas when it came to the home inspection, which we now usually did as a matter of course, so I pointed out to him on our walk that with her short coat Millie would be unlikely to get too muddy on walks.

'Oh, I'm not bothered about that,' was the response. 'I've got plenty of time to brush her afterwards, and to vacuum up. No, what's important is that she should enjoy her walks.'

Good answer.

'Would you like now to have a walk with one of the others?' I asked when we got back from the walk with Millie.

Mr Thomas smiled and shook his head.

'Are you going to come another time then to walk Millie?'

Another smile and another shake of the head. Then a pause before speaking.

'Mr Hawkins – she has stolen my heart.'

'Oh.'

The day came at last when all Mr Thomas' preparations were ready for the new member of his family to move in.

We had learnt from experience it was a good idea to give the new owner some of the food we had been feeding the dog so that an abrupt change of food wouldn't upset its tummy. As I scooped out a few days' ration Mr Thomas said, 'You know, Mr Hawkins, I don't know if this sounds silly but I feel guilty.'

I stopped what I was doing to listen.

'Both the other two dogs you showed me were lovely dogs. I feel guilty at leaving them behind. I feel I rejected them when neither of them should be rejected. And they already have been.'

I had never heard it expressed like that before by a prospective owner. It struck me what a meditative man Mr Thomas was.

'They'll be fine,' I said. 'We'll find both of them good homes.'

'Oh, don't misunderstand me, I don't have any doubts on that score. I just wish I could take them all.'

I finished scooping up dog food and handed Mr Thomas his supply.

'You know, Mr Hawkins, of all the questions you asked me, you didn't ask the one I most expected you to ask.'

Really? Oh dear. What had I forgotten? My anxiety must have registered on my face for Mr Thomas rested a hand on my arm.

'Oh, I didn't mean that as a criticism, dear man.' He paused for a moment. 'I thought you would want to know why it was that I wanted a dog, especially as I had never had one before in my life.'

It was then that Dorothy appeared with Millie. She wasn't an exuberant dog, not the sort of dog who would bound up to somebody because she was pleased to see them, but she made a bee-line across the kitchen to the man who, in getting to know her, had taken her for so many walks. She jumped up at him, in her delight standing on his polished shoes, leaving a muddy scratch mark, and a muddy streak to match on his trousers with their sharp crease. This produced a broad smile on Mr Thomas' face. He gave her a gentle pat on the head – I had the impression he wanted to make a fuss of her but wasn't sure how to react. He would learn.

Dorothy and I walked him up the drive to his car, which he had left on the road.

He nodded in the direction of the seat that overlooked the pond. 'May I sit and enjoy the view for a minute or two before I go?' he asked.

It was a surprising request. I had expected him to want to get off home. But I often myself took a few moments to sit and enjoy the setting of the village pond, overlooked by the Queen Anne farmhouse and its paddocks with horses grazing.

'I must go and walk the other dogs,' said Dorothy. She held out her hand and Mr Thomas took it and clasped it for a moment or two.

'It's been a pleasure to meet you, Mrs Hawkins,' he said. 'I will look after Millie.'

'I know you will.'

'And I'll bring her back every so often for you to see, if I may. And for you to check progress,' he added.

Dorothy gave him one of her big, kindly smiles and went off. Before she disappeared from view round the back of the cottage she turned and gave Mr Thomas and Millie a wave.

Something in the pond prompted ripples on the water, diverting Mr Thomas' attention for a few moments. Then he turned back to me.

'I'll have plenty of time on my hands to look after her, Mr Hawkins. My wife died last year and I have found that time hangs heavy. I feel that by giving a home to a dog that needs one I will be doing something useful with my empty days.' He looked down at his dog. 'And I think she is going to brighten those days for me.' He looked up again. 'Thank you.'

Mr Thomas led his dog off to his little car.

After he had driven off I stayed for a few minutes to take pleasure in the scene. Dorothy reappeared, Bo trotting happily by her side.

'Argh! Don't let that ferocious dog off!' I called out.

Dorothy unclipped his lead and Bo ran up the drive and across the green to me. He circled me twice with excitement and then sat at my feet without being asked to do so.

'You're unlucky,' I said. 'I know what you want but I haven't got any cheese on me.'

Dorothy clipped Bo's lead back on. 'That was a good one, Barrie,' she said.

'What?'

'Millie and Mr Thomas. I think that's going to be a good result for Millie and a good result for him.'

'Yeah,' I said. 'Didn't we do well?'

'We're getting on with it now, aren't we?' Dorothy said.

'That was the thirteenth we've found a home for,' I said.

'Oh.'

'You don't believe all that superstitious stuff about thirteen, do you?' I said.

'No.'

She turned to go, then paused.

'Barrie... do you remember when we homed Digby, the boy out of the breakers' yard, I said I thought it was time we had a celebration, that we should do something to celebrate having started the rescue.'

Where was this leading? 'I think I do vaguely remember something like that.'

'You said that when we had rehomed ten we would do something. Well, we've homed thirteen!'

'Bo's waiting for his walk,' I said.

'As it's Saturday, could we afford a Chinese takeaway?'

'No. This week we have had a bill from the vet's, a bill from the boarding kennels – and the size of the phone bill! I could have bought a new car with that. But we'll have one anyway.'

She turned and skipped away.

'We'll have to find you something nice to eat tonight, Bo,' she said to him, 'as we're going to be having a Chinese!'

I was longer collecting the Chinese takeaway than I had said I would be. I'd forgotten it was Saturday night and there would be a queue. And of course there was no Chinese takeaway in Wilberry. It was six miles there and six miles back for a chow mein. And I'd been late going to get it. Larry, the brown Lab cross had been sick in his pen for some reason and I'd had to clear that up. I would also have to clear up sweet and sour sauce when I got home: I'd gone round the roundabout too fast and the takeaway bag had tipped over, leaking sticky, bright red sauce onto the beige car carpet.

Nearly ten o'clock – poor Dorothy would be starving.

She wasn't in the kitchen and I carried the goodies into the living room. She was lying on the floor, her hands on her stomach.

'Have you passed out with hunger?' I asked.

'Oh, my Barrie,' she said. 'I'm in such pain.'

I dumped the takeaway down and went to her. 'Where?'

'Tummy.'

She screwed up her eyes and started to take gulps of air. She cried out suddenly and loudly. So loudly it made me jump.

'Oh. Oh. Oh.'

I was frightened. And I felt helpless.

'What can I do, sweetheart?' I said.

She shook her head, unable to speak.

'I'll ring the doctor.'

She nodded.

I grabbed the phone, dropped it, picked it up again and dialled, forcing myself to dial slowly so as not to get the wrong number.

The woman at the out-of-hours service asked questions that I could tell were to decide whether a house visit was really necessary.

'My wife isn't the sort of person to complain or make a fuss and she's lying on the floor in too much pain to get up.'

The doctor would come.

First of all I watched from the window, pulling back the curtain. Then I opened the front door and waited. Then I went and stood out on the pavement in case they couldn't find the house number.

There are lots of doctors at our practice and it was a relief to see the call taken by Dr Marshall, who remembered Dorothy and called her by her first name. She knew about Dorothy's operation. She felt Dorothy here and here and here, asked some questions, wanted Dorothy moved to the settee, gave me a kindly smile.

'I think as a precaution we should get her admitted,' she said, picking up her phone to make the call.

Hospital? I felt as if I would cry, but couldn't in front of her.

I listened to the phone call, growing more tense as I gained the impression the hospital was reluctant to take my wife. This would happen on a Saturday night when all the drunks and yobs fill casualty.

'The patient is prostrate with very severe abdominal pain,' I overheard. She went quickly through Dorothy's recent history.

'The ambulance is on its way.'

We put blankets around her to keep her warm. How long would the ambulance be?

When it arrived, kindly paramedics stretchered her out into the back of the ambulance. I felt my heart thud in my chest when they put the blue light on.

They clamped a mask on her face in the ambulance. What was it? Was it oxygen? Was it gas? I didn't want to ask the paramedic, I didn't want to distract him.

I returned home hours later to see our celebration Chinese takeaway unopened on the table.

Happy Anniversary

I was hoping to get past the nurses' station at the entrance to the ward without being noticed. The two nurses had their backs to me, conferring. I thought I'd made it. Then, eyes fixed on the two nurses, I nearly walked into a third.

'Oops, sorry!' I said.

'Hello, Mr Hawkins,' she said. 'There's a policeman been looking for your wife.'

A policeman? A flicker of anxiety. Then I guessed: Charlie.

'He's with her now,' said nurse number three and she gave me one of her big smiles I remembered from the last time Dorothy was in hospital. I remembered also she had told me her son wanted to study law and become a barrister and that she hoped he would so he could look after her in her old age.

I asked about her son. 'He's applying to Cambridge.' She raised her eyebrows to indicate her surprise.

'He'll end up a High Court Judge,' I said. She gave me that big smile again and then bustled away.

Dorothy and Charlie were sitting on the bed, chatting. Dorothy looked up as she heard me coming.

'Hello, my Barrie! It's not visiting time yet and I've already got two visitors.'

'Well, they're not going to stop Charlie, are they?' I said.

Charlie stood up and held his arm out. We shook hands. It was the first time we'd shaken hands since the day we had met – perhaps it was a gesture of solidarity as much as a greeting.

'You two will want to talk, so I won't hang about,' said Charlie.

'Charlie's only been here a few minutes,' said Dorothy.

'I've got Ivor the Terrible in the van,' Charlie said, 'And he ain't had his walk yet. And he ain't had a chance to chase anybody today either.' He put a brown paper bag on Dorothy's bedside cabinet. 'Nearly forgot – I brought you some grapes.'

My eyes met Dorothy's. 'Stay and share them with me,' she said to Charlie.

Just then a nurse appeared with some equipment. 'Time to check your blood pressure, Dorothy,' she said.

As we weren't supposed to be there I thought Charlie and I ought to disappear for a couple of minutes. Out of Dorothy's hearing Charlie said, 'She looks bright enough, doesn't she?' I took this to be his way of prompting me into telling him how she was.

'It frightened the life out of me, Charlie,' I said.

'Course it did.'

'But it's not like before. She was in hospital for over two months last year.'

Charlie pursed his lips.

'And she's coming out tomorrow. It's all to do with the op she had – apparently it's something that can happen. Something gets stuck together. Anyway, they're sure they've dealt with the problem.'

Charlie patted me on the arm. 'Well that's good.' There was a moment's pause, then he said, 'I envy you two.'

The nurse had finished taking Dorothy's blood pressure.

'You'll give me a shout if you want help, walking dogs, or anything?'

'Thanks, Charlie. But at this moment we're dogless. While Dorothy's been in here I've homed Lottie and Larry and Bo.'

'That'll help her feel better. Three in one week – you're getting good at it.'

In truth, I'd been lucky. Mr and Mrs Burton, with whom we had homed our first orphan, Monty, had decided they would like a second dog so now Monty had a playmate, Lottie, our Lurcher cross, to help him run off all that energy. And their newly married son, Paul, who we knew from when the family lived in our village, adopted our brown Lab cross, Larry.

'That Bo – you know what he was like when he came in – would you believe I homed him in Fosfen village shop?' I said. 'And there is nothing he loves more than meeting all the customers – so they can admire him and make a fuss of him.'

Charlie put a hand on my shoulder. 'You've done well.' Then he paused. 'Let's just hope one of the customers ain't that fella that pushed him under the bus.' Another pause. 'Only joking. I'll just go and say cheerio to Dorothy.'

'I'm off then,' he said to her. He took her hand, gave her a peck on the cheek and said, 'You get better. There's all them doggies out there waiting for you to rescue them.' He gave me a wave and strode off.

Dorothy watched him go. I sat down on the bed beside her. 'Has he never married?' she asked.

I shook my head. 'The topic's never come up.'

'He's a lovely man.'

'His dog thinks so,' I said. 'Although I don't suppose the yobs agree.'

Dorothy's bed was at the far end of the ward and the next three beds along were all empty, so it wasn't too noisy for us to talk.

'Dorothy, what Charlie said about getting better so you can—'

'—rescue doggies. It always makes me smile when he says "doggies". He even calls the police dogs "doggies".'

'Yes. Dorothy, you don't need me to tell you what tomorrow is, do you?'

She gave a little wriggle. 'We've two anniversaries tomorrow,' she said. 'One's my wedding anniversary and the other one is—'

'It's that other one I want to talk to you about,' I said.

'What's there to talk about?'

'Whether we're going on with it. It's not just the bills...'

'We've coped with the dogs we've had so far,' said Dorothy in an encouraging tone of voice.

'You have, you mean.'

'Well... you're a much better dog handler than you were a year ago.'

That made me laugh. 'Very tactful,' I said.

She sighed. 'But some of the people we deal with...' Her voice trailed off.

'It's the people I've been thinking about,' I said.

'Like that chap who chucked his dog out of the car. And after you'd given him a lead and a collar and told him about the training classes and—'

'Yeah... he fooled me completely. But Roxy's OK now. Dorothy, it's something else I've been thinking about.'

I went on to tell her about the caretaker and what he had said at the end of the talk I gave to the Ladies' Circle. It would come back into my head repeatedly: 'If you've got all this time to give to doing things for animals, why don't you spend your time doing things for people instead? They're more important than animals.' I had never told Dorothy what he'd said.

Her face flushed with anger.

The nurse with the big smile appeared holding a little plastic pot which she rattled.

'I've got a right assortment here for you to take, Dorothy,' she said.

Dorothy managed to smile. I watched as she took tablet after tablet with the nurse making some notes.

'Has your boy actually had his interview yet for Cambridge?' I asked the nurse.

'Tuesday,' she said and crossed her fingers.

'Wish him luck from me,' I said.

'Thank you,' she said. And I got another one of those big smiles.

When she'd gone Dorothy said, 'Hospital isn't the place to be discussing this, my Barrie... but I think you should remind yourself of somebody else who went into hospital...'

She took hold of my hand. 'Next time what that man said comes into your thoughts then you remind yourself of Sarah Phipps. Instead of his "Why don't you do things for people?" spoiling your day, remember what she said instead.'

My wife had managed to still me. There we were in that gigantic hospital with all that turmoil around us, all that activity, all those people, but in our little bit of space at the far end of the ward for several moments all was quiet. And I could hear in my thoughts the voice of Sarah Phipps. She had such courage and selfless concern: 'I'm not afraid to die, Mr Hawkins. I'm just afraid of what will happen to my dog when I do.'

Dorothy took hold of my other hand as well and gave them both a gentle squeeze. 'And I bet you that man is one of those types who doesn't do anything to help either animals or people.'

Then she rested her forehead against my forehead.

'Now let's forget about him,' she said. We've taken in eighteen homeless dogs in a year and that's what matters.'

'Seventeen,' I said. 'Jess that we got from Luke the young vet in London wasn't in need of a home – he had one, remember?'

'We didn't know that. Still, I suppose you're right. Who'd argue with a lawyer? Seventeen, then.'

'Actually...' I said, slowly, 'it will be...'

We were standing together, holding hands, our foreheads resting together, gazing down at the floor. My smiley nurse had returned to collect the little pot. 'You two all right there?' she asked.

Foreheads still stuck together we both twisted our heads and tried to nod at the nurse. That produced the biggest smile I'd seen so far and she went off.

'Twenty,' I said to Dorothy.

She pulled away from me to get a better look at my face to see if I was joking.

'Crazy Cecilia is bringing us three this afternoon...'

Dorothy compressed her lips together for a moment in thought before saying, 'Well, we've had three in one day before now.'

'They're... er... guard dogs,' I said to the floor.

This was followed by several moments of silence. I lifted my head to find that Dorothy was standing with her mouth open.

'From a... car breakers' yard,' I added.

Dorothy felt the need to sit down on her bed.

'We've had one before, don't forget,' I said. 'Orphan Number Seven, Digby. And I don't suppose there'll be any Scouts on tour this time.'

I paused, expecting Dorothy to say something but she didn't. I think she was speechless for once.

'I'll cope,' I said.

And I did. Dorothy may have been surprised when she came home the next morning to find that everything had gone smoothly.

Their owner had come with them. He was closing his car breakers' yard to look after his elderly mother and without the yard he had nowhere to keep his dogs. And they were visual guards: their presence and barking a deterrent against burglars. He'd had two, a male, Homer, and a female, Marge, and then an unplanned family. Mr

Nolan thought his lad too old to father pups at ten but his lad had other ideas. And Mr Nolan had kept the one in the litter, Bart, that was most like his dad.

Mr Nolan, Cecilia and I took the family to the boarding kennels who kindly took our orphans at a reduced fee when we needed somewhere to put a dog. They had a luxury brick-built kennel and run that held three dogs and so the family could stay together. But I wondered how difficult it was going to be to keep them together permanently, to home a family.

'Thank you for taking them, Barrie,' said Cecilia, giving me a bear hug. 'And this is for you and Dorothy.' She produced a parcel, gift-wrapped in Christmas paper. It was the first time we'd seen her since Christmas and this was our present. I left it for Dorothy to open the next morning when she came back from hospital. It was a plastic dog, a novelty, with amusing big ears and big eyes. It was in fact a pencil sharpener but I could never bring myself to insert the pencil where it was supposed to go.

That evening we were having a Chinese takeaway – a double celebration. As I sniffed the soup appreciatively I thought I heard a car door slam. We weren't expecting any visitors. I could see through the curtain a car had stopped at the end of the drive and a young male was standing looking about him. Then I saw he had a dog with him.

I sighed. 'I'd better go and see what it's about,' I said to Dorothy.

I opened the front door. A young woman had also now got out of the car, but she had her back to me.

The young man opened our gate to let the dog in. At that distance all I could see was that it was a German Shepherd, dark, a lot more black on him than usual. The dog paused and looked about him. Then he must have seen me, for he stood gazing in my direction. The young man followed him in. The dog stood staring at me for several moments, the young man watching me. I began to feel slightly uneasy – I hoped this dog was friendly. He was certainly fixing his gaze on me. Suddenly he trotted off down the drive towards me, picking up speed as he got closer. He stopped just before he got to the Volvo estate parked on the drive. He stood with one front paw held up. I do not know how long that dog and I stood each looking at the other across the few yards of the drive, but it was one of those instances where time suddenly stood still.

Was there something familiar about him? That face...?

The dog took a few more steps towards me, then hesitated. He tilted his head. Looking back on it now, I realise that his hesitation was because I had not reacted how he expected. Until then I had not recognised him.

At first, I couldn't believe who I thought it might be. It was some months since he had gone. This couldn't be the same dog...?

And then he came to me. And it was.

I dropped to my knees and put my arms around his bulky shoulders and chest.

'Friend... Friend...'

It was making me gasp.

The young man who I did not know waited for the young woman to join him, and that was Hannah, with whom we had homed Friend. So great, so incredible a transformation, for a moment at first it was only Hannah being there that convinced me this could be Friend.

But of course it was Friend. Now I could see it. This hefty, handsome male with a shining, thick coat, a wagging tail and a cold wet nose, who was licking my ear.

'Hello, you two,' said Hannah and I realised that Dorothy was standing behind me. They embraced and Hannah introduced the young man as her fiancé.

I couldn't help it. Thinking about the state he had been in, found lying on the pavement, the skeletal body, the sores, the state of his eyes, the hours I had spent sitting with him night after night in the utility room... It was all too much for me. The tears streamed down my face as I hugged him.

For a few moments I found it difficult to get my breath. Then I thought, I must pull myself together. Dorothy and Hannah were giving each other knowing smiles but the young man was gazing at me. He was big, sporty and muscular.

'You, er, must think I'm an idiot,' I said.

He shook his head and gave me a smile. 'Hannah showed me the pictures you gave her of when he first came in,' the young man said.

A blackbird landed on the lawn and Friend went off to investigate.

'He looks fantastic, Hannah,' I said. 'I cannot believe it's the same dog.'

'We never could believe our luck in finding a veterinary nurse to take him on,' Dorothy said to her. She turned to me. 'If Melissa saw him now she would say he was three or four.'

'The vet I work for thinks he's only about three,' said Hannah.

The dog that used to be a hundred years old.

'I'm afraid I've spoilt him,' Hannah said.

'Good,' I said. 'He's earned it.'

'Yes, although I shouldn't be giving him brandy ice cream,' she said. 'But it's his favourite.'

'What?!' I said in mock horror. 'Brandy ice cream? I wouldn't mind some brandy ice cream myself. In fact, I think I could do with a brandy.'

Perhaps Friend had heard the words 'brandy ice cream' for he came back to me and nudged my hand. I took hold of his pillar-box red collar to admire it. As I touched his neck I had a surprise.

'He's all wet,' I said. 'He's wet all round his neck and on his shoulder – what's he been doing?'

Dorothy, Hannah and the young man all looked at me for a moment – then burst into laughter.

What was so funny?

'It's you that's made him so wet, Barrie,' said Dorothy. 'With your tears.'

We stood on the doorstep waving goodbye.

The car disappeared from view, leaving us both with our own thoughts. Dorothy broke the silence.

'Well, we got that one right, didn't we?'

We sure did.

'I've got something for you inside,' said Dorothy.

'A present?'

'I couldn't give you a better anniversary present than you've just had.'

In the living room she held up a sheet of paper on which there were several paragraphs in her distinctive handwriting.

'Just in case we did go on with the rescue work,' said Dorothy, 'I thought it might help if we tried to make clear to ourselves what it was we were trying to do. Then if we *did* decide to continue, we would have something to guide us.'

I took the sheet of paper from her and read:

MISSION STATEMENT
Our beliefs and objectives

- We believe every dog that is brought into this world deserves to receive proper care and treatment from his or her owner.

- Every dog who comes to us is WELCOME and will be welcomed. If we are suffering pressure from workload or lack of resources we remind ourselves that this is not the fault of this dog.

- Each dog will remain with us long enough for us to get to know his or her character and ways, so as to place that dog in a home well suited to the dog and the new keeper.

- We will not home a dog where we have a lurking doubt about the suitability of the home for the dog or the dog for the home, even if we are under pressure from the lack of available homes or other resources.

- For the owner who finds him or herself unable to keep their dog, and is concerned about the dog's future, we want to provide safe hands in which to place their friend.

- We will help the new keeper by supplying information about the dog and his or her training and care.

- We will never euthanise a dog except on the advice of a veterinary surgeon.

IN MEMORY OF ELSA

We had been married long enough for me to know that writing the Mission Statement meant not only that Dorothy wanted to go on, but how committed she was.

I took the Mission Statement and pinned it up on the inside of our front door so we would be reminded of it every time we opened the door to the next orphan.

Postscript

A few weeks after Dorothy wrote the Mission Statement, we received a letter. It was from Mr Thomas, who had given a home to Millie, the World's Smallest German Shepherd dog.

4 Railway Cottages
Darrington

Sunday 23 April

Dear Mr and Mrs Hawkins,

I wanted to write and tell you how well Millie has settled in. Although I have had her only for a few months, from the very first week it was as if she had been with me for years.

She is everything you said she would be as a German Shepherd dog, and more. We have been going to training classes, which she really enjoys, to give her something to occupy that brain of hers, and to make an evening out for both of us. She loves her walks and she and I have made friends with another German Shepherd we met and his owner.

When I took Millie from you I thought I was doing her a favour in giving her a home, but I now realise it was you and she who did the favour for me. I have no wish to remarry since losing my dear wife, and our two sons are grown up and moved away, so Millie has become my wonderful companion.

By providing her with a home I feel I am doing something useful and that gives me a sense of satisfaction. I must also add that once a week Millie and I visit a friend who now lives in a care home and for many of the residents it is the highlight of their week. They make a fuss of Millie and stroke her and many of them talk to me about not just the dogs they themselves had but other pets as well.

I thank you and Millie for giving me a reason to look forward to each day.

With kindest regards,

Peter Thomas

We added to the Mission Statement one final paragraph:

- In setting out to do our work our original concern was to help the homeless dog. We have come to realise that in giving some of our time and effort to help these animals we are also doing something for the benefit of human beings. A dog can bring to a responsible keeper companionship, an incentive to healthy exercise, enjoyment and laughter. They enrich the lives of many people.

Author's Note

Barrie and Dorothy are setting up a registered charity to continue and perhaps expand the work they do. For more information about this please visit the website:

www.gsdhomefinders.org.uk

Barrie continues giving talks to groups and as an after-dinner speaker – he has improved a lot since that first talk to the Ladies' Circle! Details can be found on his website:

www.barriehawkins.net

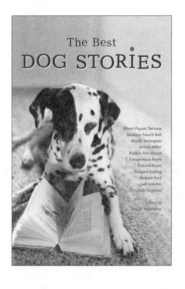